About *Quick & Healthy Volume II . . .*

"Brenda Ponichtera has done it again with *Quick & Healthy Volume II*! This cookbook and nutrition guide meets the needs of busy people who say they lack time to cook healthy meals. *Volume II* is filled with healthful and helpful food and nutrition tips, menus and shopping lists, recipes that use common ingredients easily found in the local grocery store, and best of all, recipes for good tasting family foods that can be prepared in less than 15 minutes. What more could a hungry person ask for?" ---**Nancy Clark, MS, RD, Sports Nutritionist and author of *Nancy Clark's Sports Nutrition Guidebook***

"Our customers love *Quick & Healthy Recipes and Ideas* and I know *Volume II* will delight them even more. The recipes are exactly what is claimed by the title, quick and healthy! *Volume II* is a great addition to one of my favorite cookbooks, *Quick & Healthy Recipes and Ideas*." — **Patty Merrill, Manager of Powell's Books for Cooks**

"Filled with much useful information for achieving and maintaining a healthy lifestyle. Great recipes. Highly recommended." — **John P. Foreyt, PhD, Professor, Department of Medicine, Baylor College of Medicine and author of *Living Without Dieting***

"For those just starting a low-fat lifestyle, or for those veteran health-enthusiasts in need of new recipe ideas, *Quick & Healthy Volume II* has something for everyone. The recipes offer all cooks a careful balance of creativity, health, convenience and most importantly, taste. *Quick & Healthy Volume II* lives up to its name . . . and then some!" — **Peggy Paul, RD, LD, Director, Oregon Dairy Council**

"*Quick & Healthy Volume II* provides a useful collection of convenient recipes using today's available low-fat ingredients." — **Lisë Stern, Editor, *The Cookbook Review***

"*Quick & Healthy Volume II* is a good book. It is a must for those who have the first *Quick & Healthy* and are looking for new ideas. The easy to prepare recipes are skillfully arranged and clearly written. Also, they have been well-tested so one can feel confident they will work." — **Sonja L. Connor, MS, RD, Research Associate Professor, Oregon Health Sciences University and William E. Connor, MD, Professor, Section of Clinical Nutrition, Department of Medicine, Oregon Health Sciences University; co-authors of *The New American Diet* and *The New American Diet System***

"Quick and healthy -- important for all of us, but of equal importance -- tasty and delicious. In *Volume II*, this quartet of words is combined into a melody of recipes you are sure to enjoy!" — **Marion J. Franz, MS, RD, CDE, Director of Nutrition, International Diabetes Center, Minneapolis, MN**

Quick

& Healthy

VOLUME II

*More help for people who say they don't
have time to cook healthy meals*

Brenda J. Ponichtera
Registered Dietitian

Library of Congress Catalog Card Number 91-90207

Publisher's Cataloging in Publication

Ponichtera, Brenda J.
    Quick and healthy. Vol. II, More help for people who say they don't
have time to cook healthy meals / Brenda J. Ponichtera.
        p. cm.
    Continuation of Quick and healthy recipes and ideas, 1991.
    Includes index.
    ISBN 0-9629160-1-3

    1. Low-cholesterol diet—Recipes. 2. Low-fat diet—Recipes. 3. Dia-
betes—Diet therapy—Recipes. I. Ponichtera, Brenda J. Quick
and healthy recipes and ideas. II. Title.

RM237.75.P66   641.5'63
                                QBI94-21265

Cover & Design: Lisa Drake
Art Work: Janice Staver
Typesetting: Gorge Publishing, Inc.
Editing: Mary Schlick

Printed in the United States of America
12   11   10   9   8   7   6   5   4

Published by:
ScaleDown
1519 Hermits Way
The Dalles, Oregon 97058
Phone: 541-296-5859 • Fax: 541-296-1875

to my mother,
Mary Niemic,
who has inspired me
to be the best
I can be
and
to the three special men
in my life:
my husband, Ken,
and
my sons,
Kevin and Kyle

ACKNOWLEDGEMENTS

Many people deserve to be acknowledged for their help in making this book a reality. I really appreciate their contributions.

Claudia Schon, Home Economist, helped by seeking out recipes and providing her expertise in recipe testing. I was lucky to have her on staff.

Joyce Selden was a joy to work with. She added humor to the recipe testing days and also helped with proofing.

Mary Beth Thouvenel tested all of the recipes on her family and spent considerable time proofing each recipe. Her comments were very helpful.

Beverly Rooper, Home Economist, provided recipes and helped with testing. A real pleasure to work with.

My neighbor, Arlene Cheadle, always seemed to have the ingredients we ran out of during recipe testing. She saved us many trips to the grocery store.

Several health professionals that provided input on the technical information are Peggy Paul, R.D., L.D.; Elizabeth Somer, M.A., R.D.; Connie Evers, M.S., R.D.; Nancy Clark, M.S., R.D.; Shelie Hartman-Gibbs, R.D., and Tracy Stopler Kasdan, M.S., R.D. Their comments were very useful. In addition, Jean Farmer, R.D. was invaluable in helping with the exchanges and the menus.

Jana Webb, Yvonne Lorenz, Kay Erickson, Ellie Webb and Evie Webb shared and sampled recipes and offered suggestions. I appreciate their friendship and support.

Nancy Taphouse played a key role in recipe testing and computer input. Without her, I never would have met my deadlines.

My editor, Mary Schlick, provided tremendous input. I am grateful for her help.

Artist, Janice Staver, created the drawings in this book. Her work is exceptional.

Lisa Drake, my graphic artist, is one in a million! She has the talent to transform a simple idea into a visual masterpiece. I appreciate all she has done for me.

My family deserves a special thank you for putting up with my hectic schedule. My husband, Ken, and sons, Kevin and Kyle, ate many a dinner that was a smorgasbord of leftover tested recipes. My sons and their friends also deserve a thank you for keeping me in touch with the reality of teenage appetites.

And last but not least, to the many people who used my first book and asked me to write another . . . thank you for your encouragement and enthusiasm.

TABLE OF CONTENTS

Recipes

INTRODUCTION

Healthful eating doesn't have to take a lot of time in the kitchen. With that in mind, I wrote my first book *Quick & Healthy Recipes and Ideas*. Since then, I have received many requests for more recipes and menus which is why I decided to write *Quick & Healthy Volume II*. This book contains more simple recipes, more nutrition information and more healthful tips. I think you will agree that *Volume II* will be a good addition to anyone's kitchen library.

What is quick? When testing recipes, we decided that quick meant spending less time in the kitchen. Putting together the ingredients for a meal in less than 15 minutes met that criteria. However, the cooking time can take longer since this does not usually require constant attention.

Nonfat or low-fat? When testing recipes we compared the flavor using both non-fat and low-fat products. In most cases, but not all, we preferred the low-fat. Taste is very important if your family is to continue to use a low-fat product. Keep this in mind when looking at new products and find the lower fat version, whether it be low-fat or nonfat, that your family will enjoy.

If saving time is as important to you as it is to so many, be sure to use the menus and grocery lists. Make copies of the grocery lists and keep them in a handy place in the kitchen. Encourage family members to add to the list. Keep in mind that shopping once a week, instead of several times during the week, is a real time and money saver. You'll also be pleased to know that all of the ingredients used are readily available in most grocery stores.

All of the recipes are low-fat and, when combined with other foods for the day, fall within the recommendation of no more than 20% to 30% of the total calories from fat. When a variation of a recipe is provided, the nutrition information is not listed on the recipe page unless it is very different from the original recipe. However, the complete nutrient analysis for the variation is included in the table "Nutrient Analysis of Recipes" in the back of the book.

The computer program *Nutritionist IV* and product labels were used in compiling the data for the "Nutrient Analysis of Recipes." Optional ingredients are not included in the analysis. When a choice of ingredients is listed, the first is used for the analysis.

Microwave directions are for a 700-watt microwave. Times will vary with different wattages.

Besides using the recipes in this book, be sure to look at the other helpful sections. If your goal is to eat healthfully and save time, all of the information and recipes in *Volume II* can help you reach your goal. And remember, if you have children, your example speaks louder than words.

Enjoy in good health.

Brenda J. Ponichtera
Registered Dietitian

DETERMINING IDEAL WEIGHT, CALORIES AND FAT

By following the steps below, you can find your ideal body weight, your approximate calorie needs, and the amount of fat recommended for your calorie level.

Step 1: Determine Your Ideal Body Weight
If you already know what weight is good for you, go to Step 2.

Using the table below, find your height and the corresponding weight range for your frame size.

METROPOLITAN HEIGHT AND WEIGHT TABLES
Weight in Pounds (In Indoor Clothing)*

MEN					WOMEN			
Height (In Shoes)+	Small Frame	Medium Frame	Large Frame		Height (In Shoes)+	Small Frame	Medium Frame	Large Frame
Feet Inches					**Feet Inches**			
5 2	128-134	131-141	138-150		4 10	102-111	109-121	118-131
5 3	130-136	133-143	140-153		4 11	103-113	111-123	120-134
5 4	132-138	135-145	142-156		5 0	104-115	113-126	122-137
5 5	134-140	137-148	144-160		5 1	106-118	115-129	125-140
5 6	136-142	139-151	146-164		5 2	108-121	118-132	128-143
5 7	138-145	142-154	149-168		5 3	111-124	121-135	131-147
5 8	140-148	145-157	152-172		5 4	114-127	124-138	134-151
5 9	142-151	148-160	155-176		5 5	117-130	127-141	137-155
5 10	144-154	151-163	158-180		5 6	120-133	130-144	140-159
5 11	146-157	154-166	161-184		5 7	123-136	133-147	143-163
6 0	149-160	157-170	164-188		5 8	126-139	136-150	146-167
6 1	152-164	160-174	168-192		5 9	129-142	139-153	149-170
6 2	155-168	164-178	172-197		5 10	132-145	142-156	152-173
6 3	158-172	167-182	176-202		5 11	135-148	145-159	155-176
6 4	162-176	171-187	181-207		6 0	138-151	148-162	158-179

*Indoor clothing weighing 5 pounds for men and 3 pounds for women.
+Shoes with 1-inch heels. Weights at ages 25-59.
SOURCE OF BASIC DATA: 1979 Build Study, Society of Actuaries and Association of Life Insurance Medical Directors of America, 1980. Copyright© 1983, 1993 Metropolitan Life Insurance Company

Example: Sue is 5'6" tall with a medium frame. She determines her ideal body weight to be approximately 135 pounds.

Step 2 : Choose Your Activity Level

From the table below, choose the activity level that best describes your lifestyle. Next to your activity level is the approximate number of calories you typically burn for various activities. Extremely active people will require additional calories.

CALORIE NEEDS	
Activity Level	**Calories Per Pound**
Very Active*	17
Moderately Active**	15
Inactive***	13

*__Very active:__ Daily routine includes both sitting and walking and light housework/yardwork, plus 30-60 minutes of aerobic exercise equivalent to a 3 to 4 mile brisk walk every day.

**__Moderately Active:__ Daily routine includes both sitting and walking and light housework/yardwork, plus 30-60 minutes of aerobic exercise equivalent to a 3 to 4 mile brisk walk three to four times a week.

***__Inactive:__ Daily routine includes some walking but mostly sitting; no additional exercise.

Example: Sue is a businesswoman who walks 1/2 mile to and from her office 5 times a week. In addition, she does aerobics twice a week on her lunch hour for 30 minutes.

Sue's Activity Level and Calories for Activity:

Activity Level: _Moderately Active_   Calories per Pound for Activity: _15_

Your Activity Level and Calories for Activity:

Activity Level: _____   Calories per Pound for Activity: _____

Step 3: Estimate Your Calorie Needs

Complete the formula below with the information you have so far.

Example:

	_135_ lbs	Ideal Body Weight (Step 1)
x	_15_	Calories per Pound for Activity (Step 2)
	_20.25_	Calories needed per day

Your Calorie Needs:

	_____ lbs	Ideal Body Weight
x	_____	Calories per Pound for Activity
	_____	Calories needed per day

Remember, this is only an estimate. Your actual calorie needs will vary depending upon a number of factors such as your age, body build, metabolism, and additional amount of exercise.

Adjust Calories for Weight Loss or Weight Gain

If you do not need to gain or lose weight, go to Step 4.

• **To lose weight:** Subtract 500 calories per day from your calorie needs figured above. However, it is recommended that women eat at least 1200 calories per day and that men eat a minimum of 1500 calories per day. Keep in mind that increased exercise, combined with a moderate reduction in calories is usually the best way to lose weight.

• **To gain weight:** Add 500 calories per day to your calorie needs figured above.

Example:
_20.25_ Calories – 500 Calories(for weight loss) = _15.25_ Calories needed per day
_20.25_ Calories + 500 Calories(for weight gain) = _25.25_ Calories needed per day

Adjusting Your Calories:
_____ Calories – 500 Calories(for weight loss) = _____ Calories needed per day
_____ Calories + 500 Calories(for weight gain) = _____ Calories needed per day

---

Step 4: Estimate Recommended Grams of Fat

The general recommendation for how much fat you should eat is between 20 to 30 percent of your total calories for the day. Some physicians recommend that no more than 20 percent of total calories come from fat. If your physician or registered dietitian does not tell you a specific level, the general recommendation of 20 to 30 percent is probably appropriate. Although a low-fat diet is healthy, some individuals take low-fat eating to the extreme and try to eat a no-fat diet. This is not desirable as it can interfere with the optimum balance of nutrients needed for good health.

Total fat includes saturated fat as well as monosaturated fat and polyunsaturated fat. Saturated fat intake should be limited to no more than one third of your total fat intake. Main sources of saturated fat are animal sources, palm oil, coconut oil and hydrogenated fats.

RECOMMENDED GRAMS OF FAT	
Calories per day	Grams of Total Fat (20-30% of Total Calories)
1200	27-40
1300	29-43
1400	31-47
1500	33-50
1600	36-53
1700	38-57
1800	40-60
1900	42-63
2000	44-67
2100	47-70
2200	49-73
2300	51-77
2400	53-80
2500	56-83
2600	58-87
2700	60-90
2800	62-93
2900	64-97
3000	67-100

The above table lists daily calories and the total grams of fat that represent 20% to 30% of the total calories. Using this table, find the calorie level in the first column that is closest to what you have determined in Step #3. Then, in the second column, find the amount of fat recommended for your calorie level.

Example: _2025_ Calories   _44-67_ grams of fat (20%-30% of calories)
Yours: _____ Calories   _____ grams of fat (20%-30% of calories)

Once you know how many grams of fat is reasonable for you to eat, you can compare this figure with what you are actually eating. Refer to the next section "Monitoring Fat."

MONITORING FAT

There are two easy sources for finding the grams of fat in what you eat: food labels found on almost every food product; and books and tables that list grams of fat in servings of common foods and not-so-common foods. I have included the following sections "Looking at Food Labels for Fat" and "Grams of Fat in Common Foods" to help you find the amount of fat in foods you typically eat.

After reviewing these two sections, go on to the "Sample Food Record" on page 22. Use this as a guide to complete your own food record using the form on page 23.

Make additional copies of this form; you will need one for each day. Complete your food record, listing the foods you eat in a day and the grams of fat in each food. Add up your fat grams for the day and compare it to the recommended amount you listed on page 14. Remember that your weekdays and weekends may be very different. To get a true picture, you really need to look at both.

It's natural that the amount of fat you eat will vary from day to day. However, your ultimate goal should be to keep the *average* amount of fat that you eat over a one week period within the range recommended for you.

If you are eating too much fat, refer to the section "Grams of Fat in Common Foods" on page 17, and find low-fat alternatives. Or check out the section "Trimming Fat from Your Diet" on page 28.

As you continue to look at labels, you will find more foods that are low in fat. Keep in mind that most fruits and vegetables are virtually fat-free and are good low-calorie, high-fiber choices. Your higher fat foods tend to be processed foods such as fried foods, frozen breaded products, cookies, pastries, chips and fast foods.

By keeping fat at a healthy level, you are not only protecting your cardiovascular system, but you are also keeping calories in check.

Many people have lost considerable weight by simply trimming the amount of fat they eat, and it's no secret why. Fat is more calorically dense than carbohydrate or protein. Fat has 9 calories per gram whereas carbohydrate and protein have only 4 calories per gram.

Cutting back on fat and increasing fruits and vegetables is a good way to lose weight. This has worked for many, but a low-fat diet should never be considered a free-for-all. Too many calories, whether from carbohydrate, protein, or fat, spell weight gain.

As you make changes, seek help from a registered dietitian who has the background to help you make those changes realistic for *you*.

GRAMS OF FAT IN COMMON FOODS

Below is a listing of common foods and the approximate total grams of fat for the serving size listed. Use this as a guide but be sure to read food labels as the amount of fat will vary with different brands.

FOOD	AMOUNT	GRAMS
BREADS AND GRAINS		
Bagel (2 oz.)	1	1
Bread, whole wheat, white	1 slice	1
Croissant (1.5 oz.)	1	9
Noodles/Pasta	½ cup	*
Oatmeal	1 cup	3
Pancake (4 inch diameter)	3	3
Rice, brown	½ cup	1
Tortilla, flour (7 1/2 ″)	1	2
Tortilla, corn (6 ″)	1	½
Total cereal	1 cup	1
FRUITS AND VEGETABLES		
Avocado	⅛	4
Baked potato	1 medium	*
French fries, deep fried	10	8
French fries, frozen - oven baked	10	4
Fruit: fresh, canned, or juice	½ cup	*
Vegetables: fresh, canned, or frozen	½ cup	*
BEANS (LEGUMES) AND NUTS		
Baked beans (B&M)	¼ cup	2
Garbanzo beans	¼ cup	1
Kidney beans	¼ cup	*
Pinto beans	¼ cup	*

FOOD	AMOUNT	GRAMS
Refried beans, nonfat	¼ cup	*
Soy beans	¼ cup	3
Tofu (soybean curd)	½ cup	5
Nuts: almonds, cashews, peanuts	1 oz.	13
hazelnuts/filberts, pecans, walnuts	1 oz.	18
Peanut butter, regular	1 Tbl.	8
Peanut butter, reduced fat	1 Tbl.	6
DAIRY		
Cheeses:		
Cottage cheese, regular	½ cup	5
Cottage cheese, 2%	½ cup	2
Cottage cheese, 1%	½ cup	1
Cream cheese, regular	2 Tbl.	10
Cream cheese, light	2 Tbl.	5
Cream cheese, nonfat	2 Tbl.	*
Cheddar, Swiss, American	1 oz.	9
Mozzarella, part-skim	1 oz.	5
Parmesan cheese	2 Tbl.	3
Parmesan cheese, fresh	1 oz.	7
Reduced-fat cheddar, Swiss, etc	1 oz.	5
Milk:		
Skim	1 cup	*
1%	1 cup	3
2%	1 cup	5
Whole	1 cup	8

*indicates insignificant amounts or less than ½ gram

FOOD	AMOUNT	GRAMS
Sour Cream:		
Regular	1 Tbl.	3
Light	1 Tbl.	1
Yogurt:		
Low-fat	1 cup	4
Nonfat	1 cup	*

EGGS

FOOD	AMOUNT	GRAMS
Egg, large	1	5
Egg substitute, nonfat	¼ cup	*

MEAT, POULTRY AND SEAFOOD

FOOD	AMOUNT	GRAMS
Beef:		
Ground, 9% fat (very lean)	3 oz.	12
Ground, 16% fat (very lean)	3 oz.	14
Ground, 22% fat (lean)	3 oz.	16
Ground, 27% fat (regular)	3 oz.	20
Prime rib	3 oz.	31
Top sirloin	3 oz.	5
Elk - no fat added	3 oz.	1 ½
Lamb, roast-lean only	3 oz.	8
Pork:		
Bacon, crisp	2 slices	6
Chops - loin (meat and fat)	3 oz.	22
Chops - loin (meat only)	3 oz.	10
Ham, regular	3 oz.	11
Ham, 95% fat free	3 oz.	5
Tenderloin	3 oz.	4
Poultry:		
Chicken white meat (no skin)	3 oz.	3
Chicken dark meat (no skin)	3 oz.	8

FOOD	AMOUNT	GRAMS
Fried chicken	3 oz.	15
Ground turkey, 7% fat	3 oz.	11
Turkey, white meat	3 oz.	2
Turkey, dark meat	3 oz.	6
Sausage & Sandwich Meats:		
Bologna, beef & pork	1 oz.	7
Bologna, turkey	1 oz.	5
Hot dogs, Healthy Choice brand	1	1 ½
Hot dogs, regular	1	16
Salami, beef and pork	1 oz.	5
Salami, turkey	1 oz.	4
Sandwich meat, 95% fat free	1 oz.	1
Sausage links, beef or pork	2	23
Smoked sausage & kielbasa:		
regular	3 oz.	21
low-fat turkey	3 oz.	7
Seafood:		
Crab, Shrimp, Scallops (no shell)	3 oz.	1
Clams (no shell)	3 oz.	2
Fried fish, shrimp, scallops	3 oz.	10
Oysters (no shell)	3 oz.	4
Salmon, Chinook	3 oz.	11
Tuna fish, water pack	3 oz.	1
White fillets, snapper & sole	3 oz.	1 ½
Venison - no fat added	3 oz.	3

FATS AND OILS

FOOD	AMOUNT	GRAMS
Margarine, butter, oil	1 tsp.	4
Margarine, light	1 tsp.	2
Mayonnaise, regular	1 Tbl.	11

indicates insignificant amounts or less than ½ gram

FOOD	AMOUNT	GRAMS
Mayonnaise, light	1 Tbl.	5
Mayonnaise, nonfat	1 Tbl.	*
Salad Dressings:		
Blue cheese, regular	1 Tbl..	8
Blue cheese, light	1 Tbl..	2
Italian, regular	1 Tbl.	7
Italian, fat-free	1 Tbl.	0
Ranch, regular	1 Tbl.	8
Ranch, reduced calorie	1 Tbl.	2

SNACKS AND DESSERTS

FOOD	AMOUNT	GRAMS
Apple pie	⅛ pie	12
Chips, baked tortilla	1 oz.	1
Chips (fried): potato, corn, tortilla	1 oz.	10
Chips, light potato	1 oz.	6
Cake, angel food	1 oz.	*
Cake doughnut	1	6
Chocolate chip cookie	1 small	3
Fig Bar	1	1
Gingersnaps, Graham Crackers, Vanilla wafers	2	1
Ice cream, regular	½ cup	10
Ice Milk	½ cup	3
Popcorn, no butter added:		
Air popped	3 cups	1
Popped with oil	3 cups	8
Microwave regular, popped	3 cups	6
Microwave light, popped	3 cups	1
Pretzels	1 oz.	1
Rice Cakes	1	*

FOOD	AMOUNT	GRAMS
FAST FOOD**		
Beef and Hamburgers:		
Arby's Roast Beef Sandwich, reg.	1	18
Arby's Light Roast Beef Sandwich	1	10
Cheeseburger, regular (McDonalds, Burger King)	1	14
Hamburger, regular (McDonalds, Burger King)	1	9
Wendy's Single Hamburger	1	15
McDonalds McLean Deluxe	1	10
McDonalds Quarter Pounder	1	20
McDonalds Big Mac	1	27
Burger King Whopper	1	39
Chicken:		
Burger King BK Broiler	1	29
Burger King Chicken Sandwich	1	43
Fried Chicken, drumstick & thigh	2 pieces	27
McChicken Sandwich	1	30
McDonalds McGrilled Chicken Sandwich	1	12
Egg McMuffin	1	11
Fish and Fries	2 fish & fries	28
Fish Sandwich (fried)	1	23
French Fries, small	1 order	12
Pizza, pepperoni	1 slice	11
Sausage McMuffin with Egg	1	25
Taco Bell Crisp Taco	1	11
Taco Bell Soft Chicken Taco	1	10
Taco Bell Taco Salad	1	55
Taco Bell Taco Supreme	1	15

*indicates insignificant amounts or less than ½ gram
**ordering without mayonnaise or high-fat sauces will significantly lower the fat

LOOKING AT FOOD LABELS FOR FAT

Let's look at the food label to find the total fat for one serving. Pay attention to the serving size. The amount of fat listed is based on one serving which, in many cases, may seem very small.

This is the serving size.

Total calories include calories from fat.

This is the total fat per serving. *Refer to this figure and the serving size when doing the Food Record.*

Saturated fat listed here is also included in the Total Fat.

Nutrition Facts

Serving Size ½ cup (114 g)
Servings Per Container 4

Amount Per Serving

Calories 90   Calories from Fat 30

	% Daily Value*
Total Fat 3g	5%
Saturated Fat 0g	0%
Cholesterol 0mg	0%
Sodium 300mg	13%
Total Carbohydrate 13g	4%
Dietary Fiber 3g	12%
Sugars 3g	
Protein 3g	

Vitamin A 80%	•	Vitamin C 60%
Calcium 4%	•	Iron 4%

* Percent Daily Values are based on a 2,000 calorie diet. Your daily values may be higher or lower depending on your calorie needs:

	Calories	2,000	2,500
Total Fat	Less than	65g	80g
Sat Fat	Less than	20g	25g
Cholesterol	Less than	300mg	300 mg
Sodium	Less than	2,400mg	2,400mg
Total Carbohydrate		300g	375g
Fiber		25g	30g

Calories per gram:
Fat 9 • Carbohydrate 4 • Protein 4

Calories from fat.

This is not the percent of fat in this food. This is *Percent Daily Value.*

These are Daily Values - the recommended amounts of certain nutrients for 2,000 and 2,500 calorie diets. These diets are based on 30% fat. This is the maximum. A range of 20-30% is what most health professionals recommend.

Source: Food and Drug Administration

To accurately determine the grams of fat for this food, check the serving size to see if this is the amount you typically eat. It is not unusual for people to eat two or more servings, thinking they are eating only one. At this point you may need to get out a measuring cup to be sure.

| *Example:* | 1 serving | = ½ cup | = 3 grams total fat |
| | 2 servings | = 1 cup | = 6 grams total fat |

General rule: Choose foods with less than 3 grams of fat for each 100 calories. When this is not possible, balance higher fat foods with low-fat or fat-free foods.

The percent of fat calories in one serving of food is not listed on the label. If you want to figure this, divide the total fat calories by the total calories and multiply by 100.

Example: 30 fat calories ÷ 90 total calories x 100 = 33% of calories from fat.

SAMPLE FOOD RECORD   Date: _March 6_

In addition to recording foods eaten, include fat used in cooking as well as sandwich spreads, salad dressings and anything you put on the food.

FOOD	AMOUNT	GRAMS OF FAT
orange juice	½ cup	0
oatmeal	1 cup	3
skim milk	1 cup	0
whole wheat toast	1 slice	1
fruit spread	2 tsp.	0
banana	1	0
sandwich	1	
whole wheat pita bread	1	2
water packed tuna	3 oz.	2
lettuce and tomato slices	several of each	0
light mayonnaise	2 Tbl.	10
carrot and celery sticks	5 sticks each	0
apple	1	0
Chicken Cordon Bleu (page 175)	1 serving	6
baked potato	1 small	0
light sour cream	2 Tbl.	2
broccoli	1 cup	0
Molly McButter	dash	0
tossed salad with nonfat Italian dressing	1 serving	0
garbanzo beans for salad	¼ cup	1
whole wheat roll	1	1
margarine	1 tsp.	5
skim milk	1 cup	0
chocolate chip cookies	3 small	9
light microwave popped popcorn	6 cups	2
	Total Fat:	44
	Recommended Amount:	44-67
	Difference:	0

FOOD RECORD   Date: _____

In addition to recording foods eaten, include fat used in cooking as well as sandwich spreads, salad dressings and anything you put on the food.

FOOD	AMOUNT	GRAMS OF FAT
	Total Fat:	
	Recommended Amount:	
	Difference:	

THE FOOD GUIDE PYRAMID

A simple guideline to follow for healthful eating is the Food Guide Pyramid. It consists of five major food groups and a "use sparingly" group. The pyramid illustrates that a healthy diet begins with plenty of grains, generous amounts of vegetables and fruits, and smaller amounts of meats and dairy foods. No one of the major food groups is more important than another - for good health you need them all. What matters most is that you eat a variety of foods from each group and that you balance your food choices in the proportions recommended. The fats and sugars at the top of the pyramid should be used sparingly.

THE FOOD GUIDE PYRAMID
A Guide to Daily Food Choices

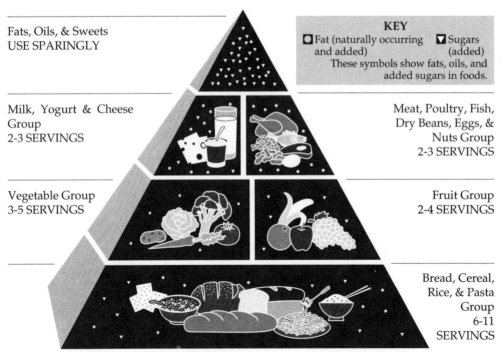

Fats, Oils, & Sweets
USE SPARINGLY

KEY
◻ Fat (naturally occurring and added) ▼ Sugars (added)
These symbols show fats, oils, and added sugars in foods.

Milk, Yogurt & Cheese Group
2-3 SERVINGS

Meat, Poultry, Fish, Dry Beans, Eggs, & Nuts Group
2-3 SERVINGS

Vegetable Group
3-5 SERVINGS

Fruit Group
2-4 SERVINGS

Bread, Cereal, Rice, & Pasta Group
6-11 SERVINGS

SOURCE: U.S. Department of Agriculture/U.S. Department of Health and Human Services

What is a serving? It isn't necessarily what you typically eat!

The chart below lists foods and serving sizes for each food group. Keep in mind that you frequently eat more than a standard serving of any one food . . . and that's okay! For example, if you were to sit down to your favorite plate of spaghetti, you may eat a total of 1 to 2 cups of pasta. This would be equal to 2 to 4 servings from the bread group because $^1/_2$ cup of cooked pasta equals 1 standard serving.

FOOD GROUPS AND SERVING SIZES*

Bread, Cereal, Rice and Pasta Group: *Choose 6-11 servings daily.*
1 slice of bread; $^1/_2$ cup cooked rice, pasta, or cereal; 1 oz. ready-to-eat cereal

Fruit Group: *Choose 2-4 servings daily.*
$^1/_2$ cup raw (chopped), cooked or canned fruit; $^3/_4$ cup fruit juice;
1 medium apple, banana, orange

Vegetable Group: *Choose 3-5 servings daily.*
1 cup of raw leafy vegetables; $^1/_2$ cup of other vegetables, cooked or raw (chopped); $^3/_4$ cup vegetable juice

Meat, Poultry, Fish, Dry Beans, Eggs and Nuts Group: *Choose 2-3 servings daily.*
2-3 ounces of cooked lean meat, poultry or fish; count the following as 1 ounce of meat: $^1/_2$ cup cooked dry beans, 1 egg or 2 tablespoons peanut butter

• *Choose lean meats - without skin - and trim all visible fat*

Milk, Yogurt and Cheese Group: *Choose 2-3 servings daily.*
1 cup of milk or yogurt; 1 $^1/_2$ ounces of natural cheese;
2 ounces of processed cheese

• *Choose nonfat or low-fat dairy products*

Fats, Oils and Sweets: *Use sparingly to limit calories and fat.*

*People with diabetes should not alter the number of servings in their meal plan without seeing *a registered dietitian. Those using the diabetes exchange lists will note that the food groups and serving sizes in the pyramid are not always the same as in the diabetes exchange lists. Some differences are:*

- *Fruit servings in the pyramid for whole fruit and juice are larger than in the diabetes exchange list.*
- *The Meat Group in the pyramid lists 2-3 ounces of meat as one serving whereas the diabetes exchange lists information for 1 ounce. However, the total ounces of meat recommended for the day are similar.*
- *Cheese is listed in the Dairy Group while in the diabetes exchange, it is listed in the Meat Group.*

HOW MANY SERVINGS DO YOU NEED EACH DAY?

	Women & some older adults	Children, teen girls, active women, most men	Teen boys & active men
Calorie level*	about 1,600	about 2,200	about 2,800
Bread group	6	9	11
Vegetable group	3	4	5
Fruit group	2	3	4
Milk group	**2-3	**2-3	**2-3
Meat group	2, for a total of 5 ounces	2, for a total of 6 ounces	3, for a total of 7 ounces

These are the calorie levels if you choose low-fat, lean foods from the major food groups and use foods from the fats, oils, and sweets group sparingly.

**Women who are pregnant or breastfeeding, teenagers, and young adults to age 24 need 3 servings.*

SOURCE: U.S. Department of Agriculture/U.S. Department of Health and Human Services

To find the number of servings that you need each day, look at the chart on the previous page. Find the category that best describes you or use the calorie needs you figured on page 13. This will give you an idea of the number of servings that you need from each food group.

While this may seem like a lot of food, most people find the recommendations make more sense once they understand serving sizes better. Take time to look at your own eating habits and count the servings that you eat in a typical day. For example, if we look at foods eaten in one day from the bread group it could look like this:

Breakfast:	1 cup cooked cereal (2 servings)
Lunch:	2 slices of bread for sandwich (2 servings)
Dinner:	1 cup noodles (2 servings)
	1 roll (1 serving)

This totals 7 servings from the bread group. Are you surprised? Most people are. It may be easier than you think to eat the pyramid way: from the base up.

Most people find that the biggest change they make in their diet when following the pyramid is to eat less meat while increasing vegetables, breads and grains. These changes can also help to reduce the fat in your diet - unless you decide to add fat to these foods.

A challenge for many people is limiting fats, oils and sweets, which are in the "use sparingly" group at the top of the pyramid. These foods do not have to be *eliminated* from your diet but they should be used in moderation as these are the extras that are high in calories but do not provide many nutrients. A good place to start limiting foods in this group is to cut back on what you add to foods in cooking and at the table. One less teaspoon of sugar on cereal or one less tablespoon of oil for a stir-fry are big steps toward eating a healthier diet.

The Food Guide Pyramid provides practical nutrition guidelines for healthy Americans. All of the major food groups are important and contribute valuable nutrients to our diet. Keep in mind that the pyramid does not replace the recommendations given by your physician or registered dietitian.

TRIMMING FAT FROM YOUR DIET

You can trim fat from your diet by using some of these ideas:

- Choose only lean meats and trim all visible fat before cooking.
- Remove the skin from chicken.
- Choose lean beef with 10% fat or less.
- Choose ground turkey with 7% fat or less.
- Look for meat that has little or no marbling of fat.
- Avoid high-fat meats such as bacon, bologna, salami.
- Avoid foods fried in oil or other fats.
- Use a nonstick cooking spray for frying.
- Saute foods in a few tablespoons of broth, fruit juice or water.
- Bake, broil, simmer, microwave or barbecue.
- Skim fat from homemade and canned soups.
- Substitute the following reduced-fat or nonfat foods for higher-fat foods:

     skim or 1% milk
     evaporated skim milk
     nonfat yogurt (plain or flavored)
     ice milk
     light or nonfat sour cream
     light or nonfat cream cheese
     reduced-fat or nonfat mayonnaise
     reduced-fat or nonfat salad dressings
     reduced-fat cheeses
     reduced-fat margarine
     nonfat tartar sauce
     water-packed tuna

• Limit use of margarine on vegetables - try a sprinkle of Molly McButter instead.

• Use a fruit spread or light cream cheese on toast instead of margarine.

• Use lettuce and tomato on sandwiches instead of mayonnaise.

• Substitute low-fat snacks for traditional high-fat snacks:
  (Look for no more than 3 grams of fat for every 100 calories)

    pretzels, both hard and soft (salt-free available)
    light microwave popcorn
    air-popped popcorn
    fresh fruit
    low-fat ice milk
    low-fat frozen yogurt
    frozen juice bars
    rice cakes
    corn cakes (caramel flavor is my favorite)
    tomato juice with a twist of lemon (salt-free available)
    raw vegetable sticks with nonfat salad dressing for a dip
    low-fat crackers and cookies
    graham crackers, vanilla wafers, gingersnaps, animal crackers, fig bars
    unsalted-top saltines
    low-fat hot cocoa
    soda pop with a scoop of low-fat ice milk

CUTTING BACK ON SODIUM

Not everyone needs to be on a low sodium diet. However, it is still prudent to limit sodium to no more than 2400 mg per day. If your doctor has prescribed a sodium restricted diet, it may be very restrictive (such as 1000 mg per day) or moderately restrictive (such as 2000 mg per day). Talk with a registered dietitian to get specific guidelines for your restriction.

We acquire a taste for salt. By consuming less salt, we can lose this acquired taste. This has happened to me and I find that I no longer like the salty taste of ham or bacon.

Processed foods often have sodium added and provide us with far more sodium than fresh foods. Limiting processed foods, limiting salt at the table, and limiting salt used in cooking are the three main ways to reduce sodium in your diet.

Here are some simple things that you can do to reduce the amount of sodium that you eat:

- Use fresh foods and limit processed foods such as convenience foods, canned foods, fast foods and most snack foods.
- Buy canned vegetables with no added salt.
- Drain and rinse vegetables canned with salt.
- Limit salted and cured meats such as ham, bacon and luncheon meats.
- Try some of the lower sodium products such as reduced-salt ham or reduced-salt bacon. Keep in mind that these still have significant amounts of sodium but less than the real thing.
- Use small amounts of regular Kikkoman soy sauce and dilute it with an equal amount of water. It has a better flavor and less sodium than the reduced-sodium soy sauce.
- Use salt-free or reduced-salt soups, broths and bouillon.

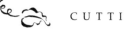

- Use seasoning powders and avoid seasoning salts. Garlic powder is a better choice than garlic salt.

- Go light on condiments such as ketchup, mustard and steak sauce.

- Try unsalted snack foods such as: unsalted, baked tortilla chips; unsalted popcorn; crackers with unsalted tops.

- Select fast foods lower in sodium by limiting pickles, cheese and salt on french fries.

- Choose reduced-fat natural brick cheese instead of processed cheese.

- Limit the amount of salt used at the table.

- Limit the amount of salt used in cooking, but keep in mind that small amounts used in cooking may provide just enough flavor to prevent you from adding twice the amount at the table.

- Make gradual instead of drastic changes. You'll find this easier to adjust to and you're more likely to stick with it.

The sodium content for each recipe in this book is listed in the "Nutrient Analysis of Recipes" in the back of the book. All of the recipes are less than 750 mg of sodium per serving with the exception of Chili Dogs and Eggplant Lasagna. These recipes include a notation for individuals on a sodium restricted diet.

EXERCISE - JUST DO SOMETHING!

What is the best kind of exercise? This is a common question I'm asked and my standard reply is the best exercise is the one you will enjoy doing on a regular basis, for 20-30 minutes, three to four times a week. But keep in mind that anything you do to get your body moving is better than nothing at all. Some of the more popular aerobic exercises - exercise that requires oxygen consumption - include walking, jogging, aerobic classes, jumping rope and use of special equipment such as a stair stepper, cross country machine and treadmill.

There are many benefits to following a consistent exercise program which incorporates aerobics, strength training and stretching. Just feeling good and being able to perform daily tasks without feeling exhausted are wonderful benefits but here are a few more to motivate you to do something:

- Decreased risk of heart disease
- Increased HDL cholesterol (the good cholesterol)
- Better control of blood pressure
- Reduced risk of osteoporosis
- Reduced depression and better mental health
- Improved blood sugar control
- Increased basal metabolic rate
- Better weight control
- Decreased body fat
- Improved quality of life

Here are some ideas to get you started:

- Do what you enjoy. If you enjoy what you are doing, there is a better chance you will continue with it.

- Get a routine going. Plan to exercise four times a week. If you miss one time you'll still have exercised three times. Exercising on a regular basis becomes a routine - like brushing your teeth - and doesn't require as much thought.

- Find a time that works for you. Look at your daily schedule and see what time of the day will have the least number of obstacles. Make it convenient for yourself.

- Set realistic goals that you can achieve. Exercising three times a week for 45 minutes may be more realistic for you than exercising every day. Too often, when unrealistic goals are set, a person just gives up.

- Ask friends to join you. Exercising with friends makes the time go by faster and it's more enjoyable. Find committed exercise companions - find several - so you'll always have someone to exercise with.

- Have an alternate plan. If you're a fair weather person and won't walk in the rain, consider walking in a mall or going to a health club. If you go to exercise classes and know you will miss one, plan on doing another kind of physical activity at a more convenient time.

- Continue to exercise while on vacation. Walking, going to a health club or tuning into an exercise program on television are all things you should think about before you go on vacation. Have a plan, even for when you are out of town.

- Have the right shoes and clothing. If you're a walker, you'll need good walking shoes and a raincoat. Sweat suits or shorts are fine for health clubs. You don't have to buy expensive outfits.

- Incorporate extra steps throughout your day. Park the car farther away, use stairs instead of elevators and walk during your break time. Every little bit counts.

- Don't put off exercising until tomorrow. Remember, tomorrow never comes.

- Consider your well-being, both physical and mental, a top priority. It's okay to take time for yourself to exercise, go on a fun outing or just to relax. Don't feel guilty!

- Have a positive attitude and you will succeed.

In addition to aerobic exercise, try to incorporate exercises that improve flexibility and also exercises that strengthen muscle and improve muscle endurance.

Stretching improves flexibility. By gradually stretching the major muscle groups, you can increase your flexibility. The main benefit is to reduce the risk of injury while involved in sports or in normal daily activities such as bending, reaching and lifting. To get more information on stretching exercises, consult a fitness trainer or a physical therapist.

Strength training makes muscles stronger and improves muscular endurance. Strength training includes lifting weights or using special equipment, such as CYBEX and Nautilus machines. Most health clubs have this type of equipment. It is easy to use but you should have the fitness trainer show you how to use it correctly. By doing these exercises you'll have more strength and endurance for doing daily activities such as carrying groceries, walking and gardening. Strength training can also improve your performance in certain sports.

Lastly, but very importantly, do consult a physician before starting any exercise program. And if you have physical limitations that prevent you from exercising, do consult a physical therapist – they can design a program to meet your special needs.

FOOD EXCHANGES
FOR DIABETES AND WEIGHT LOSS

Exchange lists or food groups are commonly used in many weight loss programs and in meal planning for people with diabetes. There are six food groups or exchange lists. In forming the exchange lists, foods with similar nutrient values are grouped together. However, the calories, carbohydrate, protein and fat used for each exchange list are averages and are not always the exact values for a specific food within the food group. The six exchange lists are: milk, starch, meat, fruits, vegetables and fat.

By following a meal pattern based on the exchange lists, one can "exchange" a food in one group for another food in the same group in the portion size listed. This method helps to increase variety while at the same time keeping calories and nutrient values consistent.

At the end of each recipe you'll find the exchanges listed. The figures used to calculate the exchanges are from the *Exchange Lists for Meal Planning* by the American Diabetes Association and the American Dietetic Association. For more information on how to use the exchanges, contact a registered dietitian or your local American Diabetes Association.

Unless otherwise noted, the calories listed for each recipe are within 30 calories of the combined caloric value of the exchanges listed after each recipe. Many of the chicken and fish recipes in this book have a notation that the calories are less than the exchanges would compute. This is because the fat content of the fish and chicken used in the recipes is lower than the fat figure (3 grams per ounce) used for the lean meat group in the exchange lists. Recipes with less than 20 calories per serving are usually listed as "free."

Sugar is used in some of the recipes and these recipes may be used by people with diabetes. However, these foods should be substituted for other carbohydrates and not simply added to the meal.

In addition to the exchanges at the end of each recipe, you'll also find calories and grams of carbohydrate, protein and fat. If you are carbohydrate counting or keeping track of grams of fat, this information will be especially useful to you.

MENUS - WEEK I

Dinner menus are listed below as well as ideas for breakfast and lunch. The corresponding grocery list is on the following page. Since breakfast and lunch routines are very individual, food items for these meals are not included on the grocery list. However, space is provided to add foods for these meals. The recipes from this book are marked with an asterisk. Although milk is not listed, it would be a good addition to any meal. Adjust portion sizes to meet your calorie needs.

Breakfast: For a balanced breakfast, include fruit or fruit juice and grains such as breads and cereals. Add low-fat dairy products and other low-fat protein-rich foods for additional nutrients. Use some of the following ideas to add variety to your breakfast:

Spanish Quiche*; nonfat yogurt with sliced fruit; Pear Custard*; peanut butter toast; assorted breads such as bagels, English muffins, hard roll, whole wheat toast and Carrot Muffins*; assorted cereals (hot and cold); fruits and fruit juices

Lunch: For a balanced lunch, include grains, vegetables and/or fruits, and low-fat protein foods from the meat group and dairy group. Refer to the Food Guide Pyramid on page 24 for additional guidelines. Use some of the following ideas to add variety to your lunch:

Beef and Cabbage Sandwich*; sandwiches with low-fat meats and cheese; tuna salad sandwich; sliced low-fat meats and cheese with sliced vegetables; melon with low-fat cottage cheese; tossed salad with garbanzo and kidney beans; leftovers, especially soups and casseroles

DINNER MENUS

Creamy Seafood Fettucini*
Fresh Asparagus
French Roll

South of the Border Lasagna*
Fruit Cocktail Salad*

Chicken Cordon Bleu*
Creamy Mashed Potatoes*
Green Bean Sauté*

Eggplant Parmesan*
Angel Hair Pasta
Tossed Salad
Nonfat Yogurt with
Fresh Fruit

Stuffed Fish Fillets*
Cheese Sauce*
Carrots (microwave)
Whole Wheat Roll

Green Chili Pork Stew*
Mexican Cornbread*

Chicken Chop Suey*
Quick-Cooking Brown Rice

WEEK I - GROCERY LIST

The size of containers listed are those specified in the recipes. Check each recipe for quantity needed.

Canned Fruits & Juices
applesauce
fruit cocktail (16 oz.)

Canned Vegetables & Sauces
bean sprouts (16 oz.)
corn, cream style (17 oz.)
corn, whole kernel (17 oz.)
green beans (16 oz.)
green chiles, diced (4 oz.)
green chiles, diced (7 oz.)
soy sauce
spaghetti sauce
    (less than 4g fat/4 oz.)
tomatoes, diced (16 oz.)

Fresh Produce
Fruits
    fresh fruit, assorted
Vegetables
    asparagus
    carrots
    celery
    eggplant
    garlic, chopped
    green onions
    lettuce
    mushrooms
    onions, yellow
    potatoes
    salad ingredients
    tomatoes

Pasta, Rice & Beans
angel hair pasta
egg noodles - "no yolk" type
rice, brown, quick-cooking

Dairy & Cheese
cheddar cheese, medium,
    reduced-fat
cheddar cheese, sharp,
    reduced-fat
cottage cheese, low-fat
egg substitute
milk, skim
mozzarella cheese, part-skim
Parmesan cheese, grated
sour cream, light
Swiss cheese, reduced-fat
yogurt, nonfat flavored

Meat, Poultry & Seafood
chicken breasts, skinless,
    boneless
fish fillets
ground beef (9% fat) or
    ground turkey (7% fat)
ham, low-fat
pork tenderloin
seafood: firm fish (cod, halibut),
    scallops, and/or shelled and
    deveined shrimp

Breads & Grains
cornflake crumbs
French rolls
stuffing, unseasoned
tortillas , corn
whole wheat rolls

Snack Foods:
_____
_____
_____
_____

Seasonings & Extracts
cayenne pepper
chili powder
cumin
dill weed, dried
garlic powder
ginger
nutmeg
parsley, dried
pepper
sage
salt (optional)
thyme, dried

Staples
baking soda
canola oil
chicken broth or instant bouillon
cornstarch
molasses
non-stick cooking spray
unbleached flour
yellow cornmeal

Miscellaneous
gelatin, sugarfree
    raspberry-flavored (0.3 oz.)
sherry, dry
salad dressing, nonfat/low-fat:
    your favorite

Breakfast & Lunch Foods:
_____
_____
_____
_____
_____

MENUS - WEEK II

Dinner menus are listed below as well as ideas for breakfast and lunch. The corresponding grocery list is on the following page. Since breakfast and lunch routines are very individual, food items for these meals are not included on the grocery list. However, space is provided to add foods for these meals. The recipes from this book are marked with an asterisk. Although milk is not listed, it would be a good addition to any meal. Adjust portion sizes to meet your calorie needs.

Breakfast: For a balanced breakfast, include fruit or fruit juice and grains such as breads and cereals. Add low-fat dairy products and other low-fat protein-rich foods for additional nutrients. Use some of the following ideas to add variety to your breakfast:

> Apple Cider Pancakes*; Sausage and Egg Casserole*; low-fat cottage cheese and fruit; Raisin Bread Pudding*; assorted cereals (hot and cold); fruits and fruit juices; assorted breads such as bagels, English muffins, hard roll, whole wheat toast and Banana Bread*

Lunch: For a balanced lunch, include grains, vegetables and/or fruits, and low-fat protein foods from the meat group and dairy group. Refer to the Food Guide Pyramid on page 24 for additional guidelines. Use some of the following ideas to add variety to your lunch:

> Canned reduced-fat turkey chili with French roll; Garden Deli Sandwich*; Ricotta Pizza*; Chicken Soup*; Tuna Macaroni Salad*; sandwiches with low-fat meats and cheese; tossed salad with garbanzo and kidney beans; leftovers, especially soups and casseroles

DINNER MENUS

Cornbread Casserole*
Sliced Cucumbers

Seafood Pasta*
Tossed Salad

Black Bean and Chicken
Casserole*
Citrus Salad*

Creamy Cabbage Soup*
Rye Bread
Mozzarella and Tomato
Salad*

Roast Chicken and
Vegetables*
Cranberry Sauce

Ginger Beef*
Quick-Cooking Brown
Rice
Grilled Eggplant*

Broiled Seafood Muffins*
Summer Cole Slaw*

WEEK II - GROCERY LIST

The size of containers listed are those specified in the recipes. Check each recipe for quantity needed.

Canned Fruits & Juices
cranberry sauce
lime juice

Canned Vegetables & Sauces
black beans (15 oz.)
green chiles, diced (4 oz.)
soy sauce
tomatoes, diced (16 oz.)

Frozen Foods
mixed vegetables

Fresh Produce
Fruits
    grapefruit
    oranges
Vegetables
    cabbage
    carrots
    celery
    cucumber
    eggplant
    garlic, chopped
    ginger root
    green onions
    lettuce
    onions, red
    onions, yellow
    potatoes
    salad ingredients
    tomatoes

Pasta, Rice & Beans
rice, brown, quick-cooking
ziti pasta - tube shape

Dairy & Cheese
cheddar cheese, medium,
    reduced-fat
egg substitute
milk, skim
mozzarella cheese, part-skim
Parmesan cheese, grated
yogurt, nonfat plain

Meat, Poultry & Seafood
chicken breasts, skinless,
    boneless
chicken, whole fryer
crab or shrimp
ground beef (9% fat) or
    ground turkey (7% fat)
seafood: firm fish (cod, halibut),
    scallops, and/or shelled
    and deveined shrimp
smoked turkey sausage
    (Polish kielbasa type,
    90% fat-free)
top sirloin steak

Breads & Grains
English muffins
rye bread

Breakfast & Lunch Foods:
_____
_____
_____
_____

Snack Foods:
_____
_____

Seasonings & Extracts
basil, dried
cayenne pepper
chili powder
cumin
garlic powder
onion powder
oregano, dried
paprika
parsley, dried
pepper
salt (optional)

Staples
baking powder
beef broth or instant bouillon
canola oil
chicken broth or instant
    bouillon
cornstarch
Dijon mustard
granulated sugar
mayonnaise, light
non-stick cooking spray
olive oil
unbleached flour
vinegar, cider
vinegar, red wine
yellow cornmeal

Miscellaneous
salad dressing, nonfat/low-fat:
    your favorite
sherry, dry

MENUS - WEEK III

Dinner menus are listed below as well as ideas for breakfast and lunch. The corresponding grocery list is on the following page. Since breakfast and lunch routines are very individual, food items for these meals are not included on the grocery list. However, space is provided to add foods for these meals. The recipes from this book are marked with an asterisk. Although milk is not listed, it would be a good addition to any meal. Adjust portion sizes to meet your calorie needs.

Breakfast: For a balanced breakfast, include fruit or fruit juice and grains such as breads and cereals. Add low-fat dairy products and other low-fat protein-rich foods for additional nutrients. Use some of the following ideas to add variety to your breakfast:

> Grapenut Pudding*; French toast (made with egg substitute); low-fat ricotta cheese and sliced fruit; assorted cereals (hot and cold); fruits and fruit juices; assorted breads such as bagels, English muffins, hard roll, whole wheat toast, Date Nut Bread* and Pineapple Bread*

Lunch: For a balanced lunch, include grains, vegetables and/or fruits, and low-fat protein foods from the meat group and dairy group. Refer to the Food Guide Pyramid on page 24 for additional guidelines. Use some of the following ideas to add variety to your lunch:

> Tuna Quesadillas*; baked potato with Cottage Cheese Topping*; Vegetable Pita Sandwich*; Spiced Tomato Broth* and sandwich; Confetti Shrimp Salad*; sandwiches with low-fat meats and cheese; tossed salad with garbanzo and kidney beans; leftovers (soups and casseroles)

DINNER MENUS

Hawaiian Chicken Salad*
French Roll
Raw Vegetable Slices

Szechuan Seafood*
Low-Fat Ramen Noodles
Cucumbers with
Dill Yogurt*

Chicken á la King*
Drop Biscuits*
Brussel Sprouts
(microwave)

Italian Curry Pasta*
Low-Fat Cottage Cheese
Sliced Fruit

Sausage and Lentil Stew*
Hot French Bread with
Pimento & Cheese
Spread*

Patio Chicken and Rice*
Orange Wedges

Oriental Pork & Noodles*
Glazed Fruit Cup*

WEEK III - GROCERY LIST

The size of containers listed are those specified in the recipes. Check each recipe for quantity needed.

Canned Fruits & Juices
lemon juice
pineapple, tidbits (15 ¼ oz.)

Canned Vegetables & Sauces
mushrooms, sliced (4 oz.)
pimento
soy sauce
szechuan sauce
teriyaki sauce
water chestnuts (8 oz.)

Frozen Foods
peas

Fresh Produce
Fruits
    fresh fruit, assorted
    oranges
Vegetables
    bell peppers: green, red,
      yellow
    broccoli
    brussel sprouts
    carrots
    celery
    cucumber
    garlic, chopped
    green onions
    onions, yellow
    potatoes
    raw vegetables, assorted
    tomatoes

Pasta, Rice & Beans
angel hair pasta
lentils
ramen noodles, low-fat
rice, brown, quick-cooking
vermicelli, coil

Dairy & Cheese
cheddar cheese, medium,
    reduced-fat
cottage cheese, low-fat
milk, skim
Parmesan cheese, grated
yogurt, nonfat plain

Meat, Poultry & Seafood
chicken or turkey, cooked &
    cubed
chicken parts (thighs, legs and
    breasts)
pork tenderloin
seafood: firm fish (cod, halibut),
    scallops, and/or shelled and
    deveined shrimp
smoked turkey sausage (Polish
    kielbasa type, 90% fat-free)

Breads & Grains
French bread
French rolls

Snack Foods:
_____
_____

Seasonings & Extracts
coriander
cumin
curry
dill weed, dried
garlic powder
ginger
onion, dried, chopped
paprika
pepper
salt (optional)

Staples
baking powder
canola oil
chicken broth or instant
    bouillon
cornstarch
granulated sugar
mayonnaise, light
non-stick cooking spray
unbleached flour
whole wheat flour

Miscellaneous
jam or jelly, sugarfree
peanuts, dry roasted, unsalted

Breakfast & Lunch Foods:
_____
_____
_____
_____
_____

MENUS - WEEK IV

Dinner menus are listed below as well as ideas for breakfast and lunch. The corresponding grocery list is on the following page. Since breakfast and lunch routines are very individual, food items for these meals are not included on the grocery list. However, space is provided to add foods for these meals. The recipes from this book are marked with an asterisk. Although milk is not listed, it would be a good addition to any meal. Adjust portion sizes to meet your calorie needs.

Breakfast: For a balanced breakfast, include fruit or fruit juice and grains such as breads and cereals. Add low-fat dairy products and other low-fat protein-rich foods for additional nutrients. Use some of the following ideas to add variety to your breakfast:

> Sausage Quiche*; hot cereal topped with nonfat yogurt; Peach Custard*; peanut butter toast; assorted cereals (hot and cold); fruits and fruit juices; assorted breads such as bagels, English muffins, hard roll, whole wheat toast and Pumpkin Bread*

Lunch: For a balanced lunch, include grains, vegetables and/or fruits, and low-fat protein foods from the meat group and dairy group. Refer to the Food Guide Pyramid on page 24 for additional guidelines. Use some of the following ideas to add variety to your lunch:

> Turkey sandwich with sliced tomato and green chiles; fruit plate with sliced low-fat cheese; Chicken Caesar Salad*; Seafood Pasta Salad*; tuna salad on a bagel; Chili Dogs*; sandwiches with low-fat meats and cheese; tossed salad with garbanzo and kidney beans; leftovers

DINNER MENUS

Cheese and Noodle Bake*
Sliced Tomatoes

Chicken Stir-Fry
Sandwich*
Waldorf Salad*

Taco Salad*

Curried Sole*
Baked Sweet Potatoes
or Yams*
Ranch-Style Vegetables*

Chicken Parmesan*
Tossed Salad

Unstuffed Cabbage
Casserole*
Focaccia Bread

Black Bean Soup*
Cheese and Chili
Quesadillas*

WEEK IV - GROCERY LIST

The size of containers listed are those specified in the recipes. Check each recipe for quantity needed.

Canned Fruits & Juices
lemon juice

Canned Vegetables & Sauces
black beans (15 oz.)
green chiles, diced (4 oz.)
kidney beans (15 1/4 oz.)
salsa, thick & chunky
spaghetti sauce
   (less than 4g fat/4 oz.)

Fresh Produce
Fruits
   apples
Vegetables
   bell peppers: green, red,
      yellow
   broccoli
   cabbage
   carrots
   cauliflower
   celery
   garlic, chopped
   green onions
   lettuce
   onions, yellow
   salad ingredients
   tomatoes
   yams/sweet potatoes

Pasta, Rice & Beans
elbow macaroni
fettucini noodles
rice, brown, quick-cooking

Dairy & Cheese
cheddar cheese, medium,
   reduced-fat
cheddar cheese, sharp,
   reduced-fat
milk, skim
mozzarella cheese, part-skim
Parmesan cheese, grated
yogurt, nonfat plain

Meat, Poultry & Seafood
chicken breasts, skinless,
   boneless
fillet of sole
ground beef (9% fat) or
   ground turkey (7% fat)

Breads & Grains
focaccia bread (16 oz.),
   whole wheat
tortillas - flour (7 1/2")
whole wheat pita bread

Seasonings & Extracts
chili powder
cumin
curry
dill weed, dried
garlic powder
onion powder
oregano, dried
parsley, dried
pepper
salt (optional)
thyme, dried

Soup & Soup Mixes
tomato soup (10 3/4 oz.)

Staples
beef broth or instant bouillon
mayonnaise, light
unbleached flour

Miscellaneous
raisins
salad dressings, nonfat/low-fat:
   ranch-style
   thousand island
   your favorite
tortilla chips, baked

Breakfast & Lunch Foods:
_____
_____
_____
_____
_____

Snack Foods:
_____
_____
_____
_____

MENUS - WEEK V

Dinner menus are listed below as well as ideas for breakfast and lunch. The corresponding grocery list is on the following page. Since breakfast and lunch routines are very individual, food items for these meals are not included on the grocery list. However, space is provided to add foods for these meals. The recipes from this book are marked with an asterisk. Although milk is not listed, it would be a good addition to any meal. Adjust portion sizes to meet your calorie needs.

Breakfast: For a balanced breakfast, include fruit or fruit juice and grains such as breads and cereals. Add low-fat dairy products and other low-fat protein-rich foods for additional nutrients. Use some of the following ideas to add variety to your breakfast:

> Applesauce Bread Pudding*; Ricotta Pizza*; scrambled eggs (substitute); nonfat yogurt with fruit and Grapenut cereal; assorted cereals (hot and cold); fruits and fruit juices; assorted breads such as bagels, English muffins, hard roll, whole wheat toast and Buttermilk Bran Breakfast Bars*

Lunch: For a balanced lunch, include grains, vegetables and/or fruits, and low-fat protein foods from the meat group and dairy group. Refer to the Food Guide Pyramid on page 24 for additional guidelines. Use some of the following ideas to add variety to your lunch:

> Black Bean Quesadillas*; Tuna Burger*; Vegetable Stir-Fry Sandwich*; Tortilla Soup* and soft taco; Turkey Reuben Sandwich*; sandwiches with low-fat meats and cheese; tossed salad with garbanzo and kidney beans; leftovers, especially soups and casseroles

DINNER MENUS

Harvest Primavera*
Italian Bread
Mandarin Cottage Salad*

Hot German Potato Salad*
Smoked Turkey Polish
Sausage (low-fat)
Sliced Tomatoes and
Cucumbers
Carrot Muffins*

Chicken Chili*
Celery and Carrot Sticks

Beef Stroganoff*
Fettucini Noodles
Fresh Cooked Broccoli

Seafood Medley*
Quick-Cooking Brown
Rice

Teriyaki Chicken Breasts*
Barbecued Potatoes*
Grilled Vegetable Medley*

Italian Baked Ziti*
Tossed Salad
Focaccia Veggie Bread*

WEEK V - GROCERY LIST

The size of containers listed are those specified in the recipes. Check each recipe for quantity needed.

Canned Fruits & Juices
applesauce
mandarin oranges (11 oz.)
pineapple, crushed (8 oz.)

Canned Vegetables & Sauces
carrots, puree (6 oz.)
green chiles, diced (4 oz.)
kidney beans (15 1/4 oz.)
mushrooms, sliced (4 oz.)
soy sauce
spaghetti sauce
   (less than 4g fat/4 oz.)
tomatoes, diced (16 oz.)

Frozen Foods
pea pods (6 oz.)
whipped topping, light

Fresh Produce
Vegetables
   bell peppers: green, red,
      yellow
   broccoli
   carrots
   celery
   cucumber
   garlic, chopped
   green onions
   onions, yellow
   potatoes
   salad ingredients
   squash, summer (yellow)
   tomatoes
   zucchini

Pasta, Rice & Beans
egg noodles - "no yolk" type
fettucini noodles
rice, brown, quick-cooking
ziti pasta - tube shape

Dairy & Cheese
cottage cheese, low-fat
egg substitute
milk, skim
Parmesan cheese, grated
sour cream, nonfat
yogurt, nonfat vanilla

Meat, Poultry & Seafood
chicken breasts, skinless,
   boneless
ground beef (9% fat) or
   ground turkey (7% fat)
seafood: firm fish (cod, halibut),
   scallops, and/or shelled and
   deveined shrimp
smoked turkey sausage (Polish
   kielbasa type, 90% fat-free)
top sirloin steak

Breads & Grains
focaccia bread (16 oz.),
   whole wheat
Italian bread
oat bran

Breakfast, Lunch & Snacks:
_____
_____
_____
_____

Seasonings & Extracts
allspice
celery seed
chili powder
cilantro, dried
cumin
garlic powder
ginger
Italian seasoning
onion, dried, chopped
onion powder
paprika
parsley, dried
pepper
salt (optional)
vanilla extract

Staples
baking powder
baking soda
beef broth or instant bouillon
brown sugar
chicken broth/instant bouillon
cornstarch
granulated sugar
non-stick cooking spray
olive oil
unbleached flour
vinegar, cider

Miscellaneous
bacon-flavor soy bits
gelatin, sugarfree
   orange flavored (0.3 oz.)
raisins, seedless
salad dressing, nonfat/low-fat:
   your favorite

MEASUREMENTS AND METRIC CONVERSIONS

STANDARD MEASURES

3 tsp	=	1 Tbl
4 Tbl	=	1/4 cup
8 Tbl	=	1/2 cup
16 Tbl	=	1 cup
2 cups	=	1 pint
4 cups	=	1 quart

WEIGHTS

U.S.		Metric
1 oz	=	28 g
2 oz	=	57 g
4 oz (1/4 lb)	=	114 g
6 oz	=	170 g
8 oz (1/2 lb)	=	227 g
12 oz (3/4 lb)	=	340 g
1 lb (16 oz)	=	454 g

LENGTH

U.S.		Metric
1 inch	=	2.54 cm
8 inches	=	20 cm
9 inches	=	23 cm
13 inches	=	33 cm

VOLUME

U.S.		Metric
1/4 tsp	=	1 ml
1/2 tsp	=	2 ml
1 tsp	=	5 ml
2 tsp	=	10 ml
1 Tbl	=	15 ml
1/4 cup (4 Tbl)	=	60 ml
1/3 cup	=	80 ml
1/2 cup (8 Tbl)	=	120 ml
2/3 cup	=	160 ml
3/4 cup	=	180 ml
1 cup (16 Tbl)	=	240 ml
2 cups	=	480 ml
4 cups (1 quart)	=	950 ml

TEMPERATURES

Fahrenheit		Celsius
325	=	165
350	=	175
375	=	190
400	=	205
425	=	220
450	=	230

Abbreviations: oz - ounce; lb - pound; tsp - teaspoon; Tbl - tablespoon; qt - quart; g - grams; ml - milliliter; cm - centimeter; l - liter

Figures based on: 1 oz = 28.35 g; 1 lb = 453.59 g; 1 Tbl = 14.8 ml; 1 cup = 237 ml

Appetizers and Sauces

Small amounts of appetizers and sauces provide variety and fit well in a healthy diet. However, keep in mind that large amounts can contribute excessive calories. So watch your portions!

Most often I prefer to use the low-fat version of cream cheese in these recipes as it has more of a cheesy flavor. However, in some recipes that have a predominant flavor from other ingredients, I find the nonfat cream cheese to be acceptable. Choose what your family prefers. However, keep in mind that the low-fat version still has a fair amount of fat so portions should be limited.

Cheese Sauce

A creamy sauce that's good on potatoes, broccoli, asparagus or cauliflower.

1 cup cold skim milk, divided
2 Tbl. unbleached flour
1/4 tsp. salt (optional)
1/8 tsp. pepper
2 oz. reduced-fat sharp cheddar cheese, cut in small pieces

Combine 1/2 cup milk with flour in covered container and shake well to prevent lumps. Pour into a 4-cup glass measuring cup along with the rest of the milk and seasonings. Cook in the microwave on high for 3 to 4 minutes, stirring with a wire whisk every 30 seconds until thickened. Add cheese and stir until melted.

Yield: about 1 cup (8 servings)
One serving: 2 tablespoons
Per serving: 40 calories, 3 grams carbohydrate, 4 grams protein, 1 gram fat
Exchanges: 1/4 milk

Variation: Dill Cheese Sauce - Add 1 1/2 tsp. of dried dill weed with seasonings.

Dijon Sauce

Try this sauce as a dip for raw cauliflower and zucchini slices or for cooked artichokes. This sauce is also good on sliced tomatoes or cucumbers.

3 Tbl. light mayonnaise
2 Tbl. cup nonfat plain yogurt
2 tsp. Dijon mustard
1 tsp. honey or the equivalent in artificial sweetener

Mix all ingredients. Use as a dip or as a dressing.

Yield: 6 tablespoons (9 servings)
One serving: 2 teaspoons
Per serving: 21 calories, 1 gram carbohydrate, 0 grams protein, 2 grams fat
Exchanges: 1/2 fat

Cottage Cheese Baked Potato Topping

Using a blender or food processor makes the cottage cheese a smooth consistency. However, that step can be omitted if the texture of cottage cheese is not objectional to you. The flavor of this topping is excellent.

2 Tbl. plain nonfat yogurt or 2 Tbl. skim milk
½ cup low-fat cottage cheese
dash of pepper
⅛ tsp. salt (optional)
⅛ tsp. onion powder
2 Tbl. chopped green onions

Mix yogurt, cottage cheese, pepper, salt (optional) and onion powder in a blender. Whip until smooth. Add green onions. Serve on baked potatoes.

Yield: ³/₄ cup (6 servings)
One serving: 2 tablespoons
Per serving: 18 calories, 1 gram carbohydrate, 3 grams protein, 0 grams fat
Exchanges: "free"

Sour Cream Baked Potato Topping

Smooth, creamy and low-fat describes this topping. A sprinkle of bacon-flavored soy bits can also be added to top the potatoes.

½ cup light sour cream
2 Tbl. nonfat plain yogurt
⅛ tsp. salt (optional)
dash of pepper
2 Tbl. chopped green onions

Mix sour cream, yogurt, salt (optional) and pepper. Add the green onions.

Yield: ³/₄ cup (6 servings)
One serving: 2 tablespoons
Per serving: 22 calories, 2 grams carbohydrate, 1 gram protein, 1 gram fat
Exchanges: "free" (or ¹/₄ skim milk)

Layered Black Bean Dip

Serve as a dip for raw vegetables such as jicama, celery, carrot sticks and pepper slices.

1 can (15 oz.) black beans, drained and rinsed
$1/4$ tsp. onion powder
$1/4$ tsp. dried oregano
$1/8$ tsp. garlic powder
$1/8$ tsp. cayenne pepper
$1/2$ cup salsa, thick and chunky
$1/2$ cup light sour cream
$1/4$ cup chopped green onions
2 oz. grated reduced-fat cheddar cheese

Mash beans and mix with onion powder, dried oregano, garlic powder and cayenne pepper. Spread on a serving dish. Top with salsa, sour cream, green onions and grated cheese.

Yield: 2 cups (16 servings)
One serving: 2 tablespoons
Per serving: 38 calories, 4 grams carbohydrate, 3 grams protein, 1 gram fat
Exchanges: $1/2$ starch

SPANISH BEAN DIPS

These two variations are great with baked tortilla chips that you can now find in grocery stores. Also, try these high-fiber dips with raw veggies. Garnish with chopped green onion and chopped tomatoes for color.

Bean and Salsa Dip

The salsa flavor is apparent is this dip. Use a hot salsa if you dare.

1 can (16 oz.) vegetarian or nonfat refried beans
1/2 cup salsa, thick and chunky

Mix all ingredients in a microwave-safe bowl. Cover and cook on high until hot (about 1 minute), stirring several times during cooking.

Yield: 2 cups (16 servings)
One serving: 2 tablespoons
Per serving: 24 calories, 5 grams carbohydrate, 1 gram protein, 0 grams fat
Exchanges: 1/3 starch

Bean and Cheese Dip

The cream cheese adds a little variety to this dip. Keep in mind that it also adds fat, so use sparingly. We have chosen the light cream cheese instead of the nonfat cream cheese because we think it has a better flavor in this recipe.

1 can (16 oz.) vegetarian or nonfat refried beans
1/2 cup light cream cheese
1/4 cup salsa, thick and chunky

Mix all ingredients in a microwave-safe bowl. Cover and cook on high until hot (about 1 minute), stirring several times during cooking.

Yield: 2 cups (16 servings)
One serving: 2 tablespoons
Per serving: 39 calories, 5 grams carbohydrate, 2 grams protein, 1 gram fat
Exchanges: 1/2 starch

Chili Cheese Dip

This dip is popular at parties. Watch your portion size as the calories can easily add up. We have chosen the light cream cheese instead of the nonfat because we think it has a better flavor in this recipe. However, many find the flavor of the nonfat cream cheese acceptable.

1 can (15 oz.) reduced-fat turkey chili with beans*
¹/₂ cup light cream cheese

Mix all ingredients in a microwave-safe bowl. Cover and cook on high until hot (about 1 minute), stirring several times during cooking.

Yield: 2 cups (16 servings)
One serving: 2 tablespoons
Per serving: 40 calories, 3 grams carbohydrate, 3 grams protein, 2 grams fat
Exchanges: ¹/₃ starch, ¹/₃ lean meat

*or choose a chili with no more than 8 grams of fat per 220 calories

Cream Cheese Spread

Use as a dip for vegetables or spread on cucumber or zucchini slices.

8 oz. tub nonfat cream cheese, at room temperature
¹/₂ cup light sour cream
1 Tbl. dried onion
1 Tbl. dried parsley
1 tsp. dried basil
¹/₄ tsp. each: dried thyme & garlic powder
¹/₈ tsp. pepper

Mix all ingredients.

Yield: about 1 ¹/₂ cups (24 servings)
One serving: 1 tablespoon
Per serving: 13 calories, 1 gram carbohydrate, 1 gram protein, 0 grams fat
Exchanges: "free"

Cucumber Spread

Use as a spread on cocktail bread, cucumber slices, or on celery sticks.

8 oz. tub nonfat cream cheese, at room temperature
1 cup finely chopped cucumber
6 green onions, minced
2 Tbl. light sour cream
1/8 tsp. pepper

Mix all ingredients.

Yield: 2 cups (16 servings)
One serving: 2 tablespoons
Per serving: 13 calories, 1 gram carbohydrate, 2 grams protein, 0 grams fat
Exchanges: "free"

Herbed Cream Cheese

Try this wonderful spread. It can be used as a party spread or at lunch time on bagels. We liked the flavor of the light cream cheese instead of the nonfat cream cheese in this recipe.

8 oz. tub light cream cheese, at room temperature
2 Tbl. light mayonnaise
1 tsp. lemon juice
1 tsp. chopped garlic
1/2 tsp. onion powder
1/2 tsp. Italian seasoning

Mix all ingredients together. Serve spread on bagels, crackers, toast, cucumbers, zucchini, celery and other crisp foods.

Yield: 1 cup (16 servings)
One serving: 1 tablespoon
Per serving: 39 calories, 1 gram carbohydrate, 1 gram protein, 3 grams fat
Exchanges: 1/2 medium-fat meat

Pimento and Cheese Spread

Simple and tasty, this spread can be used on vegetables, crackers or bread.

1 jar (2 oz.) pimento
4 oz. grated reduced-fat cheddar cheese
¼ cup light mayonnaise
⅛ tsp. garlic powder

Mix all ingredients.

For a hot appetizer, spread on French bread and broil until cheese is melted.

For a cold appetizer, arrange sliced vegetables and crackers on a platter around a bowl of the spread. Or make individual canapés by placing a small amount on vegetable slices such as zucchini and cucumber.

Yield: 1 cup (16 servings)
One serving: 1 tablespoon
Per serving: 34 calories, 1 gram carbohydrate, 2 grams protein, 2 grams fat
Exchanges: ½ lean meat

Tuna Paté

Serve with vegetables or spread on crackers. Garnish with fresh parsley.

8 oz. tub nonfat cream cheese, at room temperature
2 cans (6 ⅛ oz. each) water-packed tuna, drained and flaked
2 Tbl. chili sauce
2 tsp. dried parsley
1 tsp. minced onion
4 drops Tabasco sauce

In a blender, blend all ingredients until smooth.

Yield: 2 cups (16 servings)
One serving: 2 tablespoons
Per serving: 34 calories, 1 gram carbohydrate, 7 grams protein, 0 grams fat
Exchanges*: 1 lean meat

*Due to the low fat content of tuna fish, the calories are less than the exchanges would compute.

Veggie Spread

This spread takes on the flavor of the vegetables that you add. Serve on zucchini or cucumber slices or use as a dip for carrots and celery.

8 oz. tub nonfat cream cheese, at room temperature
⅓ cup light mayonnaise
1 tsp. dried dill weed
1 tsp. dried parsley
½ tsp. garlic powder
½ tsp. dried basil
1 cup assorted finely chopped vegetables (such as bell peppers, carrots, celery, cauliflower, etc.)

Mix cream cheese, mayonnaise, dried dill weed, dried parsley, garlic powder and dried basil. Blend until smooth. Add chopped vegetables, reserving a few to sprinkle over the top. Serve as a spread for cocktail bread or unsalted top crackers.

Yield: 2 cups (16 servings)
One serving: 2 tablespoons
Per serving: 28 calories, 2 grams carbohydrate, 2 grams protein, 1 gram fat
Exchanges: ¼ lean meat, ½ vegetable

Breads

Breads and grains provide the foundation for a healthful diet. To save time when preparing some of the breads in this section, double the recipe and freeze one loaf for later use.

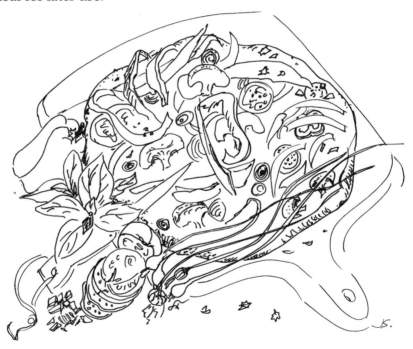

Apple Cider Pancakes

Cider gives these a good apple flavor. Try serving with hot applesauce sprinkled with cinnamon.

¼ cup old fashioned oats
1 cup pancake mix (no more than 3g of fat per ½ cup mix)
¾ cup apple cider

Spray a griddle or skillet with non-stick cooking spray. With a wire whisk, blend all ingredients until smooth. Pour slightly less than ¼ cup of batter per pancake on a hot griddle or skillet. Cook about 1 to 1 ½ minutes per side or until golden.

Yield: 8 pancakes (4 servings)
One serving: 2 pancakes
Per serving: 144 calories, 30 grams carbohydrate, 4 grams protein, 1 gram fat
Exchanges: 2 starch

Banana Bread

Use ripe bananas in this fat-free bread. Serve as a breakfast bread or as a dessert with a dollop of light whipped topping. I use an 8″ x 8″ pan instead of a loaf pan because it cooks more uniformly.

½ cup granulated sugar
¼ cup unsweetened applesauce
½ cup egg substitute (equal to 2 eggs)
¼ cup skim milk
1 cup mashed banana
¾ cup unbleached flour
¾ cup whole wheat flour
½ cup oat bran
2 tsp. baking powder
½ tsp. ground cinnamon
¼ tsp. baking soda
¼ tsp. ground nutmeg
¼ tsp. salt (optional)

Preheat oven to 350 degrees. Spray an 8″ x 8″ pan with non-stick cooking spray. In a large mixing bowl, combine sugar, applesauce, egg substitute, milk and banana. In a separate bowl, mix remaining ingredients. Add dry ingredients to the banana mixture. Stir just until flour is moistened. Pour into pan and bake for 50-55 minutes or until toothpick inserted in the center comes out clean.

Yield: 9 servings
One serving: ¹/₉ recipe
Per serving: 166 calories, 35 grams carbohydrate, 5 grams protein, 1 gram fat
Exchanges: 2 starch

Buttermilk Bran Breakfast Squares

This is a variation of the popular buttermilk muffin recipe from my first book. Amounts are reduced to make nine servings. It's very moist, high in fiber and low-fat.

½ cup boiling water
½ cup All Bran cereal
¼ cup egg substitute (equal to 1 egg)
1 cup buttermilk
½ cup sugar
¼ cup unsweetened applesauce
¾ cup whole wheat flour
½ cup unbleached flour
1 tsp. baking soda
½ tsp. salt (optional)
1 cup Bran Buds or 100% Bran cereal

Preheat oven to 350 degrees. In a small bowl, pour boiling water over the All Bran cereal and let stand until softened. In a large bowl, mix egg substitute, buttermilk, sugar and applesauce. Add the All Bran/water mixture to the egg mixture. Stir in flours, baking soda and salt (optional). Mix just until moistened. Stir in Bran Buds or 100% Bran cereal.

Pour into an 8" x 8" pan that has been sprayed with non-stick cooking spray. Bake for 55-60 minutes or until a toothpick inserted into the center comes out clean. Cut into 9 servings.

Yield: 9 servings
One serving: ⅑ recipe
Per serving: 169 calories, 35 grams carbohydrate, 5 grams protein, 1 gram fat
Exchanges: 2 starch

Carrot Muffins

These fat-free muffins taste great. Serve for breakfast or as a snack.

1 ³/₄ cups unbleached flour
³/₄ cup sugar
¹/₂ cup oat bran
1 tsp. baking soda
1 tsp. allspice
¹/₂ tsp. salt (optional)
¹/₂ tsp. baking powder
2 jars (6 oz. each) pureed carrots (baby food type)
¹/₂ cup egg substitute (equal to 2 eggs)
¹/₂ cup unsweetened applesauce
¹/₂ cup seedless raisins
1 tsp. vanilla extract

Preheat oven to 350 degrees. Spray muffin tins with non-stick cooking spray. In a medium bowl, combine flour, sugar, oat bran, baking soda, allspice, salt (optional) and baking powder. In a larger bowl, mix carrots, with remaining ingredients until well-blended. Stir flour mixture into carrot mixture just until flour is moistened. Spoon batter into muffin tins. Bake for 30 minutes or until toothpick inserted in the center comes out clean.

Yield: 12 muffins
One serving: 1 muffin
Per serving: 163 calories, 36 grams carbohydrate, 4 grams protein, 0 grams fat
Exchanges: 2 starch

Date Nut Bread

This recipe, contributed by our own recipe tester, Joyce Selden, won a blue ribbon at the Wasco County Fair. Consider doubling this recipe and making two loaves. Freeze one for later use.

5 oz. dates, chopped (about 1 cup)
1 tsp. baking soda
1 cup hot coffee
1 cup sugar
¼ cup egg substitute (equal to 1 egg)
1 Tbl. canola oil
1 tsp. vanilla
⅛ tsp. salt (optional)
2 cups unbleached flour
½ cup chopped nuts

Preheat oven to 350 degrees. Mix dates with baking soda and coffee. Set aside to cool. Mix in sugar, egg substitute, canola oil, vanilla and salt (optional). Add flour and stir just until flour is moistened. Fold in nuts. Pour into a 9" x 5" x 3" loaf pan that has been sprayed with non-stick cooking spray. Bake for 55-60 minutes or until a toothpick inserted in the center comes out clean.

Yield: 16 slices
One serving: 1 slice
Per serving: 156 calories, 32 grams carbohydrate, 3 grams protein, 2 grams fat
Exchanges: 2 starch

Pineapple Bread

This high fiber coffee cake is fat-free and has a distinct pineapple flavor. A good choice for breakfast. I used an 8″ x 8″ pan instead of a loaf pan because it cooked more uniformly. This is a heavy textured bread compared to most quick breads because of the "healthy" ingredients. Also consider this as a dessert cake.

¾ cup unbleached flour
¾ cup whole wheat flour
½ cup oat bran
½ cup brown sugar
2 tsp. baking powder
½ tsp. cinnamon
½ tsp. salt (optional)
½ tsp. baking soda
1 can (8 oz.) crushed pineapple (in juice), not drained
½ cup egg substitute (equal to 2 eggs)
¼ cup unsweetened applesauce

Preheat oven to 350 degrees. Spray an 8″ x 8″ pan with non-stick cooking spray. Blend dry ingredients. Mix remaining ingredients in a separate bowl. Stir into flour mixture just until flour is moistened. Pour into pan. Bake 40-45 minutes, or until toothpick inserted in the center comes out clean.

Yield: 9 servings
One serving: ¹/₉ recipe
Per serving: 158 calories, 33 grams carbohydrate, 5 grams protein, 1 gram fat
Exchanges: 2 starch

Pumpkin Bread

The spices used in this nonfat bread compliment the pumpkin flavor. I use an 8" x 8" pan instead of a loaf pan because it cooks more uniformly. The texture of this bread is heavier than most quick breads because of the "healthy" ingredients. Also consider this for dessert with a dollop of light whipped topping and a sprinkle of nutmeg.

1 cup unbleached flour
³/₄ cup whole wheat flour
³/₄ cup sugar
¹/₂ cup oat bran
1 tsp. baking soda
¹/₂ tsp. salt (optional)
¹/₂ tsp. baking powder
¹/₂ tsp. allspice
¹/₂ tsp. cinnamon
¹/₂ tsp. ground cloves
1 cup canned pumpkin
¹/₂ cup egg substitute (equal to 2 eggs)
¹/₂ cup unsweetened applesauce
1 tsp. vanilla extract

Preheat oven to 350 degrees. Spray an 8" x 8" pan with non-stick cooking spray. In a medium bowl, combine dry ingredients. In a larger bowl, mix pumpkin with remaining ingredients until well-blended. Stir flour mixture into pumpkin mixture just until flour is moistened. Pour into pan. Bake for 55-60 minutes or until toothpick inserted in the center comes out clean.

Yield: 9 servings
One serving: ¹/₉ recipe
Per serving: 187 calories, 40 grams carbohydrate, 5 grams protein, 1 gram fat
Exchanges: 2 ¹/₂ starch

Drop Biscuits

These are quick to prepare and taste so good, it's hard to believe they are low in fat. Use as an accompaniment to breakfast or dinner. Also, you can serve these as a dessert shortcake with sliced fruit and light whipped topping.

1 ½ cups unbleached flour
½ cup whole wheat flour
1 Tbl. sugar
1 Tbl. baking powder
¼ tsp. salt (optional)
1 cup skim milk
2 Tbl. canola oil

Preheat oven to 400 degrees. Spray a baking sheet with non-stick cooking spray. Mix dry ingredients. Gradually stir in milk and oil, mixing with a fork until the mixture leaves the sides of the bowl. Drop by spoonfuls onto the baking sheet, making 8 biscuits. Bake for 15 minutes or until golden brown.

Yield: 8 biscuits (8 servings)
One serving: 1 biscuit
Per serving: 165 calories, 27 grams carbohydrate, 5 grams protein, 4 grams fat
Exchanges: 2 starch, ½ fat

Variations:

Traditional Biscuits - Add an additional 1-2 Tbl. of flour so that the dough is firm enough to handle. Divide dough into 8 pieces and, with your hands, form into 8 biscuits. Bake as for drop biscuits.

Biscuit Wedges - Add an additional 1-2 Tbl. of flour so that the dough is firm enough to handle. Divide dough into 2 pieces and pat out to form two flat circles, about 6" in diameter, on the baking sheet. Score with a knife to form 8 wedges each. Bake for 15-20 minutes. Top each wedge with 1 teaspoon sugar-free jam or jelly (spreadable fruit) before serving.

Optional Toppings - Sprinkle with grated Parmesan cheese and/or Italian seasoning before baking.

Bread Sticks

If you like bread sticks but don't want to take the time to make them from scratch, try this simple recipe that uses frozen bread dough. To save time, I prefer to thaw a loaf in the refrigerator overnight.

1 loaf (1 lb.) frozen whole wheat bread dough, thawed according to package directions
¼ cup egg substitute (equal to 1 egg)

Preheat oven to 375 degrees. Lightly coat a baking sheet with non–stick cooking spray. Cut bread dough into 12 equal pieces. With your hands, stretch and form each piece into a 7″ rope. Place on baking sheets. Brush with egg. Sprinkle with optional ingredients (listed below) if desired. Set aside to rise in a warm, draft-free location until doubled in size, about 1 hour.

Bake 10 minutes, until golden brown. Immediately remove bread sticks from baking sheet.

Optional Ingredients: Before baking, sprinkle with 1 teaspoon of one of the following:
caraway seed
poppy seed
sesame seed
grated Parmesan cheese
Italian seasoning

Yield: 12 bread sticks (12 servings)
One serving: 1 bread stick
Per serving: 106 calories, 18 grams carbohydrate, 5 grams protein, 1 gram fat
Exchanges: 1 starch, ½ fat

Focaccia Cheese Bread

Use store-bought Focaccia for this cheesy bread. Serve with soup or pasta dishes.

1 lb. loaf whole wheat Focaccia bread
2 oz. reduced-fat sharp cheddar cheese, cut in small cubes
½ Tbl. pesto sauce <u>or</u> 1 tsp. olive oil and 1 tsp. dried basil

Preheat oven to 350 degrees. Cut cheese in ¼" cubes and poke into the top of the bread. Brush with pesto sauce <u>or</u> olive oil and basil. Bake for 15-20 minutes or until golden brown.

Yield: 16 servings
One serving: ¹/₁₆ bread
Per serving: 87 calories, 13 grams carbohydrate, 4 grams protein, 2 grams fat
Exchanges: 1 starch

Focaccia Veggie Bread

This store-bought Focaccia bread takes on a delicious flavor with the addition of chopped fresh vegetables.

1 lb. loaf whole wheat Focaccia bread
1 tsp. olive oil
1 tsp. Italian seasoning
1 green onion, chopped
¼ cup diced green bell pepper
½ Tbl. grated Parmesan cheese

Preheat oven to 350 degrees. Brush bread top with olive oil and sprinkle with Italian seasoning. Press onion and pepper into the top of the bread. Sprinkle with cheese. Bake for 15-20 minutes or until golden brown.

Yield: 16 servings
One serving: ¹/₁₆ bread
Per serving: 77 calories, 13 grams carbohydrate, 3 grams protein, 2 grams fat
Exchanges: 1 starch

Mexican Cornbread

You'll find this recipe different than traditional cornbread. Serve hot or cold. It is very moist and you may prefer to eat it with a fork. Try serving this with fish.

1 can (17 oz.) cream style corn*
1/2 cup egg substitute (equal to 2 eggs)
1 cup yellow corn meal
3/4 cup skim milk
3 Tbl. canola oil
1/2 tsp. baking soda
1/2 tsp. salt (optional)
1 can (4 oz.) diced green chiles
2 oz. reduced-fat cheddar cheese, grated

Preheat oven to 400 degrees. Mix all ingredients and pour into an 8" x 8" pan that has been sprayed with non-stick cooking spray. Bake for 35-40 minutes or until a toothpick inserted in the center comes out clean.

Yield: 9 servings
One serving: 1/9 recipe
Per serving: 169 calories, 22 grams carbohydrate, 6 grams protein, 6 grams fat
Exchanges: 1 1/2 starch, 1 fat

*Sodium is figured for salt-free.

Soups & Stews

There's nothing quite as good as a hot bowl of soup on a cold winter day. Soups can be good low-fat choices especially if you use fat-free broth. Skim the fat from broth, whether homemade or canned, to make it fat-free. Refrigerate soups for several hours and the fat will harden and can be easily removed. Many of the recipes in this section can become a complete meal with the addition of a bread or a salad. Plan on having the leftovers for lunch.

Sherried Broth

Try this served in a mug as an accompaniment to a sandwich on a cold winter day or as a hot drink in the evening. Chicken or vegetable broth can be substituted for beef.

1 cup beef broth, fat removed*
2 Tbl. dry sherry

Mix ingredients in a mug. Heat on high in microwave until hot and bubbly, about 2-3 minutes.

Yield: 1 serving
One serving: 1 cup
Per serving: 18 calories, 2 grams carbohydrate, 5 grams protein, 0 grams fat
Exchanges: "free"

*Sodium is figured for salt-free.

Tortilla Soup

This is a great first course to a Mexican meal. It is also a good choice for lunch on a cold day.

4 cups chicken broth, fat removed*
1 medium tomato, chopped
4 green onions, chopped
3 corn tortillas, cut into eighths

In a medium saucepan, mix broth, tomato and onion. Cover and bring to a boil. Reduce heat to low. Add tortillas and simmer, covered, for 15 minutes.

Yield: 5 cups (4 servings)
One serving: 1 1/4 cups
Per serving: 77 calories, 11 grams carbohydrate, 6 grams protein, 1 gram fat
Exchanges: 1/2 starch, 1 vegetable

*Sodium is figured for salt-free.

Spiced Tomato Broth

Serve this hot soup in a mug. It is good served with a sandwich or as a hot drink on a cold winter day.

1 cup tomato juice*
1 cup beef broth, fat removed*
3 black peppercorns
2 whole cloves
½ bay leaf
1 Tbl. lemon juice

Mix all ingredients in a saucepan. Cover and heat to boiling. Reduce heat to low and simmer for 10 minutes. Discard peppercorns, cloves, and bay leaf before serving.

Yield: 2 cups (2 servings)
One serving: 1 cup
Per serving: 41 calories, 7 grams carbohydrate, 3 grams protein, 0 grams fat
Exchanges: 1 vegetable

*Sodium is figured for salt-free.

Black Bean Soup

Serve this thick soup on a cold winter day with French bread or biscuits.

1 cup chopped onion
³/₄ cup chopped celery
2 tsp. chopped garlic
1 ¹/₂ cups beef broth, fat removed*
2 cans (15 oz. each) black beans, drained and rinsed
1/2 cup salsa, thick and chunky
1 ¹/₂ tsp. cumin
¹/₂ tsp. onion powder
¹/₄ tsp. dried oregano

Combine all ingredients in a saucepan. Cover and simmer for 20-25 minutes or until vegetables are tender.

Yield: 5 cups (4 servings)
One serving: 1 ¹/₄ cups
Per serving: 171 calories, 30 grams carbohydrate, 11 grams protein, 1 gram fat
Exchanges: 1 ¹/₂ starch, ¹/₂ lean meat, 1 vegetable

*Sodium is figured for salt-free.

Creamy Cabbage Soup

This is an excellent recipe for cabbage. It has a wonderful flavor and a creamy texture.

1 small head of cabbage (about 1 lb.)
1 medium onion, chopped
4 oz. turkey smoked sausage (Polish kielbasa type, 90% fat free), sliced
4 cups chicken broth, fat removed*
³/₄ cup cold skim milk
¹/₄ cup unbleached flour
¹/₈ tsp. pepper

Chop cabbage. Combine cabbage, onion, sausage and chicken broth in a large saucepan. Simmer until vegetables are tender. Combine cold milk with flour in covered container and shake well to prevent lumps. Stir into soup along with pepper. Heat until bubbly.

Yield: 7 ¹/₂ cups (5 servings)
One serving: 1 ¹/₂ cups
Per serving: 121 calories, 15 grams carbohydrate, 11 grams protein, 2 grams fat
Exchanges: ¹/₂ starch, 1 lean meat, 1 vegetable

*Sodium is figured for salt-free.

Garden Minestrone

This is a colorful, hearty soup that can be enjoyed year-round. Take advantage of the summer vegetables and serve this for a quick supper. You can also make this soup without the ground beef. Plan on freezing leftovers for another meal.

1 lb. extra lean ground beef (9% fat) or ground turkey (7% fat)
6 cups beef broth, fat removed*
2 cups chopped cabbage
1 can (16 oz.) diced tomatoes, not drained*
1 can (16 oz.) green beans, not drained*
1 cup sliced carrots
1 cup sliced zucchini
1 cup dry elbow macaroni
2 Tbl. dried chopped onion
2 Tbl. dried parsley
1 Tbl. chopped garlic
1 tsp. dried basil
½ tsp. dried oregano
¼ tsp. pepper

Brown meat in a 4-quart kettle that has been sprayed with non-stick cooking spray. Add remaining ingredients and simmer until vegetables are tender, about 20 minutes.

Yield: 9 cups (6 servings)
One serving: 1 ½ cups
Per serving: 302 calories, 29 grams carbohydrate, 24 grams protein, 10 grams fat
Exchanges: 1 starch, 2 medium-fat meat, 3 vegetable

*Sodium is figured for salt-free.

Venus De Milo Soup

This is a hearty soup which is great on a cold winter day. You can substitute quick-cooking barley, rice or noodles for the orzo (orzo is pasta that looks like rice). This recipe makes a large amount so you can have leftovers for lunch or freeze for another meal.

1 lb. extra lean ground beef (9% fat) or ground turkey (7% fat)
3 cups water
5 cups beef broth, fat removed*
1 large onion, chopped
1 pkg. (16 oz.) frozen mixed vegetables
1 can (16 oz.) stewed tomatoes, not drained*
1 can (8 oz.) tomato sauce*
¼ tsp. salt (optional)
⅛ tsp. pepper
¾ cup uncooked orzo or quick-cooking barley
1 Tbl. grated Parmesan cheese

In a large pot that has been sprayed with non-stick cooking spray, brown meat. Add all but the orzo and Parmesan cheese. Bring to a boil. Reduce heat to low, cover and simmer for 20-25 minutes. Add orzo and cook for 15 minutes. Serve with a sprinkling of Parmesan cheese.

Yield: 11 cups (7 servings)
One serving: about 1 ½ cups
Per serving: 293 calories, 32 grams carbohydrate, 22 grams protein, 9 grams fat
Exchanges: 1 starch, 2 medium-fat meat, 3 vegetable

*Sodium is figured for salt-free.

Oven Beef Stew

This recipe may take a while to cook but it doesn't require any attention once it's in the oven. This is a good dish to make on a Saturday afternoon and then have the leftovers during the week.

2 lbs. round steak, cut in cubes
1 medium onion, chopped
1 large stalk celery, sliced
2 medium, unpeeled potatoes, cubed
2 carrots, sliced
2 Tbl. tapioca
2 Tbl. dried parsley
$\frac{1}{2}$ tsp. dried oregano
$\frac{1}{2}$ tsp. salt (optional)
$\frac{1}{4}$ tsp. garlic powder
$\frac{1}{8}$ tsp. pepper
1 bay leaf
1 $\frac{1}{2}$ cups tomato juice*
1 cup water

Preheat oven to 325 degrees. Mix all ingredients in a 4-quart Dutch oven. Cover and bake for 2 $\frac{1}{2}$ hours.

Yield: 8 cups (8 servings)
One serving: 1 cup
Per serving: 220 calories, 23 grams carbohydrate, 23 grams protein, 4 grams fat
Exchanges: 1 starch, 2 $\frac{1}{2}$ lean meat, 1 vegetable

*Sodium is figured for salt-free.

Sausage and Lentil Stew

This thick stew is great on a cold winter day. Serve with French bread to complete the meal.

2 cups lentils
5 ½ cups water
2 medium onions, chopped
4 potatoes, cubed
2 carrots, sliced
4 tsp. chopped garlic
½ lb. turkey smoked sausage (Polish kielbasa type, 90% fat free), sliced

Rinse lentils. In a 4-quart saucepan, mix all ingredients. Bring to a boil, then reduce heat and simmer for 30 minutes or until lentils are tender.

Yield: 11 cups (11 servings)
One serving: 1 cup
Per serving: 228 calories, 40 grams carbohydrate, 13 grams protein, 2 grams fat
Exchanges: 2 starch, 1 lean meat, 1 vegetable

Green Chile Pork Stew

A great dish for a cold winter day.

1 lb. boneless pork tenderloin
1 medium onion, chopped
³/₄ cup sliced celery
2 carrots, sliced
2 medium unpeeled potatoes, cubed
1 can (7 oz.) diced green chiles
2 tsp. chopped garlic
1 cup chicken broth, fat removed*
1 cup water (or enough to cover)
2 Tbl. cornstarch
¹/₄ cup water
salsa, thick and chunky (optional)

Cut pork into 1 ¹/₂ inch cubes. In a 3-quart saucepan, mix pork with the vegetables and chicken broth. Add water to cover. Cover and simmer about 45 minutes. Mix cornstarch with remaining water. Add to stew and cook until bubbly. Serve as is or topped with a spoonful of salsa.

Yield: 7 ¹/₂ cups (5 servings)
One serving: 1 ¹/₂ cups
Per serving: 269 calories, 36 grams carbohydrate, 23 grams protein, 3 grams fat
Exchanges: 1 ¹/₂ starch, 2 lean meat, 2 vegetable

*Sodium is figured for salt-free.

Seafood Gumbo

If you like seafood and tomatoes, you'll like this Southern stew. Serve with French bread to complete the meal.

1 can (28 oz.) stewed tomatoes, not drained*
1/2 cup chopped onion
1 pkg. frozen okra (8 oz.) or 1 1/2 cups sliced celery
2 cups chicken or beef broth, fat removed*
1 tsp. chopped garlic
1 tsp. paprika
1/8 tsp. cayenne pepper
1 drop Tabasco sauce
3 Tbl. unbleached flour
1/2 cup water
1 lb. seafood such as firm fish fillets, scallops and/or shelled and deveined shrimp

In a medium saucepan, mix vegetables, broth and seasonings. Simmer, covered, until vegetables are tender. Combine flour and water in a covered container and shake well to prevent lumps. Add to simmering vegetables and cook until bubbly. Add seafood and continue to cook until seafood is done.

Yield: about 8 cups (5 servings)
One serving: about 1 1/2 cups
Per serving: 163 calories, 14 grams carbohydrate, 23 grams protein, 2 grams fat
Exchanges**: 2 1/2 lean meat, 2 vegetable

*Sodium is figured for salt-free.

**Due to the low fat content of fish, calories are less than the exchanges would compute.

Chicken Chili

Chili lovers will enjoy this thick chili. It is so simple and tasty.

½ lb. skinless, boneless chicken breasts
1 medium onion, chopped
2 tsp. chopped garlic
2 cans (15 ¼ oz. each) kidney beans, drained*
1 can (16 oz.) diced tomatoes, not drained*
1 can (4 oz.) diced green chiles
½ cup water
1 Tbl. dried cilantro
2 tsp. chili powder
½ tsp. cumin

Cut chicken in bite-size pieces. Brown chicken in a saucepan that has been sprayed with non-stick cooking spray. Add remaining ingredients. Cover and simmer for 30 minutes or until chicken is tender.

Yield: 6 cups (4 servings)
One serving: 1 ½ cups
Per serving: 296 calories, 42 grams carbohydrate, 26 grams protein, 3 grams fat
Exchanges**: 2 starch, 2 ½ lean meat, 2 vegetable

*Sodium is figured for salt-free.

**Due to the low fat content of chicken breasts, calories are less than the exchanges would compute.

Chicken Pasta Stew

A great dish for a cold winter day.

1 lb. skinless, boneless chicken breasts, cut in 1-inch pieces
1 medium onion, chopped
³/₄ cup sliced celery
1 can (7 oz.) diced green chiles
2 tsp. chopped garlic
2 cups chicken broth, fat removed*
1 cup water
4 oz. egg noodles - "no yolk" type (about 2 cups dry)
1 ¹/₂ cups frozen mixed peas and carrots

In a 3-quart saucepan, mix chicken with all but the noodles and mixed vegetables. Simmer, covered, for 15 minutes. Add remaining ingredients. Simmer, uncovered, 15 minutes or until noodles are tender.

Yield: 8 cups (5 servings)
One serving: about 1 ¹/₂ cups
Per serving: 223 calories, 25 grams carbohydrate, 25 grams protein, 3 grams fat
Exchanges**: 1 starch, 2 ¹/₂ lean meat, 2 vegetable

*Sodium is figured for salt-free.

**Due to the low fat content of chicken breasts, calories are less than the exchanges would compute.

Chicken Soup

This will remind you of real homemade chicken soup but without all the work. It's great on a cold winter day with a hot roll.

4 oz. skinless, boneless chicken breasts, cut in bite-size pieces
5 cups chicken broth, fat removed*
²/₃ cup sliced celery
½ cup sliced carrot
¼ cup chopped onion
1 Tbl. dried parsley
½ cup frozen peas
2 oz. medium-size sea shell pasta (about 1 cup dry)

In a medium saucepan, combine chicken with broth, celery, carrots, onion and parsley. Simmer, covered, until vegetables are soft. Add peas and pasta. Cook about 15 minutes or until pasta is tender.

Yield: 6 cups (4 servings)
One serving: 1 ½ cups
Per serving: 142 calories, 18 grams carbohydrate, 15 grams protein, 1 gram fat
Exchanges**: 1 starch, 1 ½ lean meat, 1 vegetable

*Sodium is figured for salt-free.

**Due to the low fat content of chicken breasts, calories are less than the exchanges would compute.

*V*egetables

The recipes in this section provide ways to prepare vegetables creatively for the whole family to enjoy. Some are prepared in the microwave, some barbecued and some are cooked on the stove. All are quick to prepare.

Using the microwave to cook fresh vegetables is another simple method that brings out their good flavor. Consult a microwave cookbook for a table of basic cooking times.

Cucumbers with Dill Yogurt

The addition of dill gives these cucumbers a distinct flavor that we found to be very appealing.

2 Tbl. nonfat plain yogurt
2 Tbl. light mayonnaise
1/2 tsp. dried dill weed
1/8 tsp. salt (optional)
2 medium cucumbers, sliced (about 2 cups)

Mix yogurt, mayonnaise and seasonings. Gently toss with cucumbers. Refrigerate to chill thoroughly.

Yield: 2 cups (4 servings)
One serving: 1/2 cup
Per serving: 35 calories, 3 grams carbohydrate, 1 gram protein, 2 grams fat
Exchanges: 1/2 vegetable, 1/2 fat

Cucumbers with Onions and Sour Cream

The combination of onions with cucumbers seems to be a favorite for many. Also, the red onions add to the flavor as well as to the eye appeal of this dish.

2 Tbl. light sour cream
2 small cucumbers, sliced
1/2 red onion, sliced very thin and cut in quarters
1/8 tsp. pepper
1/8 tsp. salt (optional)

Mix sour cream, cucumber and onion. Add seasonings. Refrigerate to chill thoroughly.

Yield: 2 cups (4 servings)
One serving: 1/2 cup
Per serving: 21 calories, 3 grams carbohydrate, 1 gram protein, 1 gram fat
Exchanges: 1 vegetable

Variation: Mild onions, also known as sweet onions, can be substituted for red onions.

Tomatoes with Yogurt Dressing

Add variety to tomatoes with this simple dressing.

1 Tbl. nonfat plain yogurt
1 Tbl. light mayonnaise
1/8 tsp. garlic powder
1/8 tsp. dried basil
1/8 tsp. salt (optional)
2 medium tomatoes, cut in bite-size pieces

Mix yogurt, mayonnaise and seasonings. Gently toss with tomatoes. Refrigerate to thoroughly chill.

Yield: 2 cups (4 servings)
One serving: 1/2 cup
Per serving: 35 calories, 6 grams carbohydrate, 1 gram protein, 1 gram fat
Exchanges: 1 vegetable

Barbecued Corn on the Cob

Richard Cutler, my cousin's husband, introduced me to this simple way of cooking corn. The outside of the husks will blacken slightly but the corn will be excellent.

4 ears of corn

Start barbecue grill. When hot, place <u>unshucked</u> corn directly on grill over high heat. Close hood and cook for 15 minutes turning corn several times while cooking. Remove corn and let sit until cool enough to handle. Pull down husks and use as a handle.

Yield: 4 servings
One serving: 1 ear of corn
Per serving: 136 calories, 28 grams carbohydrate, 4 grams protein, 1 gram fat
Exchanges: 2 starch

Barbecued Vegetable Kabobs

Try these vegetables threaded on a skewer and barbecued. They are a great accompaniment to any barbecued meat. To prevent wooden skewers from burning, soak them in water 10 minutes before using.

2 cups fresh vegetables, cut in bite-size pieces, such as: bell peppers (red, yellow, green), whole mushroom caps, zucchini and summer squash

Start the barbecue. Thread vegetables on skewers. When the grill is hot, place skewers on the grill. Cover and cook for 10 minutes, turning halfway through cooking time.

Yield: 4 servings
One serving: $1/4$ recipe
Per serving: 23 calories, 4 grams carbohydrate, 1 gram protein, 0 grams fat
Exchanges: 1 vegetable

Variation: Pineapple chunks can be alternated with the vegetables.

Barbecued Zucchini

The flavor of this barbecued zucchini is so good, even people who don't like zucchini will like this recipe.

2 small zucchini (about 5" long)
$1/4$ tsp. Italian seasoning

Start the barbecue grill. Slice the zucchini in half, lengthwise. When the barbecue is hot, place zucchini on the grill. Sprinkle with Italian seasoning. Close the hood and cook the zucchini 15 to 20 minutes, turning over halfway through cooking.

Yield: 4 servings
One serving: $1/2$ zucchini
Per serving: 12 calories, 2 grams carbohydrate, 1 gram protein, 0 grams fat
Exchanges: $1/2$ vegetable

Grilled Eggplant

This is a simple and delicious way to prepare eggplant.

1 small eggplant (about 1 lb.), peeled
2 tsp. olive oil
¼ tsp. garlic powder
⅛ tsp. salt (optional)
1 Tbl. grated Parmesan cheese

Cut eggplant into slices ¾ inch thick. Brush both sides with olive oil. Proceed with either method listed below.

Stove Top: Spray a large skillet or griddle with non-stick cooking spray. Place eggplant on the hot griddle and sprinkle with garlic powder and salt (optional). Cook about 4 minutes on each side or until tender. Remove from griddle and sprinkle with Parmesan cheese before serving.

Barbecue: *Spray a piece of aluminum foil, large enough to hold the slices, with non-stick cooking spray and place on the barbecue grill. Start barbecue. When hot, place eggplant slices on aluminum foil. Sprinkle with garlic powder and salt (optional). Close the hood and cook the eggplant 8 minutes, turning slices over halfway through cooking time. Remove from barbecue and sprinkle with Parmesan cheese before serving.

Yield: 4 servings
One serving: ¼ recipe
Per serving: 62 calories, 7 grams carbohydrate, 2 grams protein, 3 grams fat
Exchanges: 1 vegetable, ½ fat

*Note: Non-stick cooking spray is flammable. Do not spray near open flame or heated surfaces.

Grilled Vegetable Medley

This is the best recipe for zucchini that I have tried and it is also colorful. The outdoor grill gives these vegetables an excellent smoked flavor everyone will enjoy. This recipe can also be prepared in a skillet.

2 small zucchini (about 5″ long)
2 small onions (about 2″ in diameter)
1 red bell pepper
⅛ tsp. onion powder
⅛ tsp. garlic powder
⅛ tsp. paprika
dash of pepper
⅛ tsp. salt (optional)

Prepare vegetables by cutting zucchini, onions and peppers in large bite-size pieces. Sprinkle seasonings on vegetables and toss to coat evenly. Proceed with either method listed below.

Barbecue: *Spray a sheet of aluminum foil about 12″ x 12″ with non-stick cooking spray. After spraying the foil, set it on the barbecue grill. Start the grill at this point. When the barbecue is hot, arrange vegetables on the foil. Close the hood and cook for 15 minutes, turning the vegetables with a spatula halfway through the cooking time.

Stove Top: Spray a large skillet or griddle with non-stick cooking spray. Place vegetables on the hot griddle and sprinkle with seasonings. Stir-fry about 10-15 minutes or until vegetables are tender.

Yield: about 2 ½ cups (4 servings)
One serving: ¼ recipe
Per serving: 29 calories, 6 grams carbohydrate, 1 gram protein, 0 grams fat
Exchanges: 1 vegetable

*Note: Non-stick cooking spray is flammable. Do not spray near open flame or heated surfaces.

Barbecued Potatoes

What a simple way to add variety to potatoes. By using the outdoor barbecue, your kitchen stays cool on a hot summer day. You can use baking potatoes instead of new potatoes, but be sure to cut into eighths. These have a great barbecued flavor.

1 lb. small new potatoes, cut in quarters (about 4 cups)
1/8 tsp. paprika
1/8 tsp. pepper
1/8 tsp. salt (optional)

*Spray a sheet of aluminum foil about 12" x 12" with non-stick cooking spray. Set the foil on the barbecue grill. Start the grill at this point.

Add potatoes to a covered glass casserole and sprinkle with seasonings. Microwave, on high, for 5 minutes, stirring after 1 1/2 minutes. Set aside. When the barbecue is hot, arrange potatoes on the foil. Close hood and cook for 15 minutes, turning the potatoes halfway through cooking time. These have a great barbecued flavor.

Yield: 4 servings
One serving: 1/4 recipe
Per serving: 126 calories, 29 grams carbohydrate, 3 grams protein, 0 grams fat
Exchanges: 2 starch

*Note: Non-stick cooking spray is flammable. Do not spray near open flame or heated surfaces.

Creamy Mashed Potatoes

You'll find this to be a flavorful way to serve mashed potatoes. Although the dill is optional, we highly recommend it.

3 medium potatoes (about 1 lb.)
¼ cup light sour cream
¼ cup skim milk
1 Tbl. dried parsley
1 tsp. dried dill weed (optional)
¼ tsp. salt (optional)
⅛ tsp. pepper

Scrub potatoes and cut in quarters. Place in a medium saucepan and cover with water. Bring to a boil. Reduce heat and simmer until potatoes are tender, about 15 minutes. Drain. Mash potatoes, adding sour cream, milk and seasonings. Continue to mash until no longer lumpy.

Yield: 2 cups (4 servings)
One serving: ½ cup
Per serving: 146 calories, 30 grams carbohydrate, 4 grams protein, 1 gram fat
Exchanges: 2 starch

Oven Fried Parmesan Potatoes

The addition of seasonings and cheese adds flavor and a golden color to these low-fat French fries.

4 medium potatoes (about 5 oz. each)
1 Tbl. canola oil
1 Tbl. grated Parmesan cheese
½ tsp. garlic powder
½ tsp. paprika
⅛ tsp. pepper
salt to taste (optional)

Preheat oven to 450 degrees. Scrub potatoes, but don't peel. Cut in wedges or strips. Place potato slices in a plastic bag with the oil and shake well to coat potatoes evenly. In a plastic bag, mix seasonings. Add potatoes and shake to coat. Arrange potatoes, in a single layer, on a baking sheet that has been sprayed with non-stick cooking spray. Bake for 30-35 minutes or until golden brown.

Yield: 5 servings
One serving: ⅕ recipe
Per serving: 159 calories, 29 grams carbohydrate, 3 grams protein, 3 grams fat
Exchanges: 2 starch

Baked Sweet Potatoes or Yams

Use yams or sweet potatoes as a pleasant substitute for traditional baked potatoes. Both yams and sweet potatoes have a slightly sweet taste. Yams have a bright orange pulp which gives more eye appeal than the sweet potatoes which have a mustard-colored pulp. Sweet potatoes tend to take longer to cook than yams.

2 medium yams or sweet potatoes

Scrub yams with a brush and pierce skins with a fork. Proceed with oven or microwave method below.

Conventional Oven: Preheat oven to 400 degrees. Bake on a rack for 45-60 minutes or until soft when pierced with a fork.

Microwave Oven: Arrange in a microwave at least 1″ apart. Microwave on high for 9-11 minutes. Turn potatoes and rotate ¼ turn halfway through cooking time. Flesh should be soft when pierced with a fork. Let sit for 5 minutes.

Yield: 4 servings
One serving: ½ sweet potato or yam
Per serving: 60 calories, 14 grams carbohydrate, 1 gram protein, 0 grams fat
Exchanges: 1 starch

Hash Browns

If you've avoided hash browns because of the high fat content, try this fat-free version. It's great served with one of the breakfast quiches in this book.

2 cups frozen hash brown potatoes
¹/₄ tsp. salt (optional)
¹/₈ tsp. pepper

Preheat oven to 425 degrees. Spray an 8" x 8" baking pan with non-stick cooking spray. Spread the potatoes in the pan and sprinkle with seasonings. Bake for 20 minutes, turning after 10 minutes.

Yield: 2 servings
One serving: 1 cup
Per serving: 60 calories, 13 grams carbohydrate, 2 grams protein, 0 grams fat
Exchanges: 1 starch

Green Bean Sauté

This recipe dresses up a can of green beans.

1 cup chopped onion
1 cup sliced mushrooms
1 tsp. minced garlic
1 can (16 oz.) cut green beans, drained*

Spray a skillet with non-stick cooking spray. Sauté onions, mushrooms and garlic. Add green beans and heat thoroughly.

Yield: 3 cups (6 servings)
One serving: ¹/₂ cup
Per serving: 27 calories, 5 grams carbohydrate, 1 gram protein, 0 grams fat
Exchanges: 1 vegetable

*Sodium is figured for salt-free.

Italian Green Beans

This is a simple but flavorful way to dress up green beans. You can easily substitute stewed tomatoes (drained) for the fresh.

1 Tbl. dried chopped onion (or ⅓ cup sliced green onion)
2 Tbl. water
½ green bell pepper, chopped
1 can (16 oz.) green beans, drained*
1 tomato, chopped
¼ tsp. dried basil
⅛ tsp. dried rosemary

If using dried onion, soak in 2 Tbl. of water for a few minutes. Mix all ingredients in a covered microwave-safe dish. Heat on high in the microwave for 3 minutes, stirring halfway through cooking time, or until green pepper is tender.

Yield: 3 cups (6 servings)
One serving: ½ cup
Per serving: 26 calories, 5 grams carbohydrate, 1 gram protein, 0 grams fat
Exchanges: 1 vegetable

*Sodium is figured for salt-free.

Harvest Vegetable Stir-Fry

Take advantage of vegetables in season when making this recipe and substitute whatever is plentiful. Although the serving size is listed as one-half cup, you'll probably want seconds.

¹/₂ cup chopped onion
1 cup chopped green bell pepper
1 cup diced peeled eggplant
1 cup sliced zucchini
1 cup yellow summer squash, sliced
1 cup chopped tomatoes
1 tsp. Italian seasoning
¹/₄ tsp. salt (optional)
2 Tbl. grated Parmesan cheese

Spray a large skillet with non-stick cooking spray. Add onion and bell pepper and stir-fry over medium-high heat for 2 to 3 minutes. Stir in eggplant, zucchini and yellow squash. Stir-fry for 4 to 5 minutes. Stir in tomatoes and seasonings. Heat thoroughly. Sprinkle with Parmesan cheese before serving.

Yield: 4 cups (8 servings)
One serving: ¹/₂ cup
Per serving: 36 calories, 6 grams carbohydrate, 2 grams protein, 1 gram fat
Exchanges: 1 vegetable

Ranch-Style Vegetables

Any combination of fresh vegetables can be used in this dish, so keep this in mind when you're overloaded with garden vegetables.

1 cup cauliflower, bite-sized pieces
1 cup broccoli, bite-sized pieces
³/₄ cup sliced carrots
¹/₂ cup sliced celery
¹/₃ cup chopped onion
¹/₄ tsp. dried dill weed
1 ¹/₂ Tbl. lemon juice
2 Tbl. nonfat or reduced-fat ranch-style dressing

Fill a 1 ¹/₂ quart casserole, or microwave-safe dish, with vegetables. Add dill and lemon juice. Follow directions below for microwave or conventional oven.

Microwave Oven: Cover and microwave 5 to 8 minutes or until vegetables are done to your liking. Be sure to stir vegetables every 2 minutes. Drain. Mix in dressing.

Conventional Oven: Preheat oven to 350 degrees. Cover and bake 20-30 minutes until vegetables are done to your liking. Drain. Mix in dressing.

Yield: 2 cups (4 servings)
One serving: ¹/₂ cup
Per serving: 49 calories, 10 grams carbohydrate, 2 grams protein, 0 grams fat
Exchanges: 2 vegetable

Zucchini Garden Casserole

The addition of Italian dressing adds a zing to this dish. This also makes a great meatless dinner.

1 large zucchini, sliced
2 large tomatoes, chopped
1/2 red bell pepper, chopped
1/2 green bell pepper, chopped
1/4 cup nonfat Italian dressing
1 cup quick-cooking brown rice, uncooked
1 Tbl. grated Parmesan cheese (optional)

Spray a 2-quart covered casserole, or microwave-safe dish, with non-stick cooking spray. Add vegetables and dressing. In the microwave, cook on high for 10 minutes, stirring after every 3 minutes. Meanwhile, cook rice according to package directions, omitting butter and salt. Serve the vegetables with rice, spooning the juices over the rice. Sprinkle with Parmesan cheese (optional).

Yield: 4 cups of vegetables and 2 cups of rice (4 servings)
One serving: 1 cup of vegetables and 1/2 cup rice
Per serving: 149 calories, 30 grams carbohydrate, 4 grams protein, 1 gram fat
Exchanges: 1 starch, 2 vegetable

Black Bean Stuffed Peppers

This makes a great side dish or it can be served in a larger portion for a main dish. Any color of peppers work well in this recipe but the red peppers are especially attractive. A combination of red, green and yellow peppers can be used to create an eye-catching display.

3 bell peppers (about 6 oz. each)
1 can (15 oz.) black beans, drained and rinsed
1 can (8 oz.) whole kernel corn, drained*
1 cup cooked quick-cooking brown rice
¼ cup chopped green onions
1 tsp. cumin
1 tsp. garlic powder
¼ tsp. salt (optional)
⅛ tsp. cayenne pepper
2 oz. grated reduced-fat cheddar cheese

Preheat oven to 350 degrees. Cut peppers in half lengthwise and remove seeds and membranes. Place in a 9" x 13" pan that has been sprayed with non-stick cooking spray. Set aside. In a large bowl, combine remaining ingredients except cheese. Fill each pepper half with bean mixture. Pour ¼ cup water into the pan. Cover with aluminum foil and bake for 30 minutes. Sprinkle with cheese and return to oven, uncovered, for 5 minutes until cheese is melted. For smaller portions, cut each pepper half in half with a serrated knife before serving.

Yield: 6 halves (6 servings)
One serving: 1 pepper half
Per serving: 160 calories, 26 grams carbohydrate, 8 grams protein, 2 grams fat
Exchanges: 1 ½ starch, ½ lean meat, 1 vegetable

*Sodium is figured for salt-free.

Salads

Side dish as well as main dish salads are included in this section. If some of your family members don't like cooked vegetables, serve salads and raw vegetables more often.

If you don't have the time or inclination to clean lettuce and other fresh vegetables, be sure to check out the produce section in the grocery store for rinsed and ready-to-use vegetables. A real time saver!

Citrus Salad

This unusual salad is great with Mexican food. The addition of fruit gives this salad an interesting and refreshing taste.

1 grapefruit, peeled
1 orange, peeled
1 ½ quarts of greens
1 small red onion, sliced thin
2 Tbl. cider vinegar
1 Tbl. lime juice
1 Tbl. salad oil
1 Tbl. water
¼ tsp. pepper
¼ tsp. cumin
⅛ tsp. salt (optional)

Cut fruit in bite-size pieces. Toss with lettuce and onion. Mix remaining ingredients for dressing. Drizzle over salad and toss just before serving.

Yield: 8 cups (5 servings)
One serving: about 1 ½ cups
Per serving: 96 calories, 14 grams carbohydrate, 2 grams protein, 3 grams fat
Exchanges: ½ fruit, 1 vegetable, ½ fat

Frozen Fruit Salad

This is a refreshing treat for a hot summer day. Try serving this for lunch with low-fat cottage cheese.

1 can (15 ¼ oz.) pineapple tidbits, in natural juice
¼ cup sugar (or the equivalent in artificial sweetener)
1 can (11 oz.) mandarin oranges, drained
1 pkg. (8 oz.) frozen unsweetened strawberries, sliced
1 can (16 oz.) apricot halves, drained
2 bananas, sliced

Drain pineapple, reserving the liquid. Add water to the pineapple juice to equal 1 cup and add sugar, stirring until dissolved. Add all ingredients to the juice. Cover and freeze for several hours or overnight. Let sit out about 30 to 45 minutes before serving.

Yield: 6 cups (12 servings)
One serving: ½ cup
Per serving: 80 calories, 19 grams carbohydrate, 1 gram protein, 0 grams fat
Exchanges: 1 ½ fruit

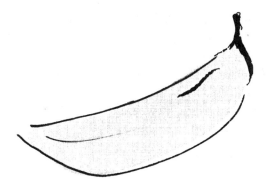

Fruit Cocktail Salad

You'll find this to be an attractive dish that can be served on lettuce leaves for a salad or in sherbet glasses for dessert.

1 can (16 oz.) fruit cocktail, in juice
1 small pkg. (0.3 oz.) sugar-free raspberry flavored gelatin
1 cup applesauce, unsweetened

Drain fruit cocktail reserving the juice. Add water to the juice to equal 1 cup. Bring to a boil. Dissolve gelatin in the boiling water/juice mixture. Add remaining ingredients. Chill until set.

Yield: 3 cups (6 servings)
One serving: $1/2$ cup
Per serving: 57 calories, 13 grams carbohydrate, 1 gram protein, 0 grams fat
Exchanges: 1 fruit

Mandarin Cottage Salad

This light dish has a refreshing taste and a pretty pastel orange color.

2 cups low-fat, small curd cottage cheese
1 can (11 oz.) mandarin orange sections, drained
1 can (8 oz.) crushed pineapple (packed in juice), drained
2 pkg. (0.3 oz. each) sugar-free, orange flavored gelatin
1 cup light whipped topping
8 oz. vanilla nonfat yogurt, sweetened with artificial sweetener

Mix all ingredients. Cover and refrigerate until serving.

Yield: 5 cups (6 servings)
One serving: about $3/4$ cup
Per serving: 131 calories, 14 grams carbohydrate, 13 grams protein, 2 grams fat
Exchanges: $1/2$ milk, 1 lean meat, $1/2$ fruit

Waldorf Salad

You'll find this to be a Fall favorite when apples are plentiful. This is a good alternative to traditional green salads.

3 Tbl. light mayonnaise
2 Tbl. skim milk
2 cups diced apples, unpeeled
2 tsp. lemon juice
1 cup diced celery
¼ cup raisins

Mix mayonnaise and milk until smooth. Toss apples with lemon juice. Add remaining ingredients and mayonnaise mixture. Toss to coat.

Yield: about 3 cups (6 servings)
One serving: ¹/₂ cup
Per serving: 73 calories, 12 grams carbohydrate, 1 gram protein, 2 grams fat
Exchanges: 1 fruit, ¹/₂ fat

Broccoli Salad

This is a variation of a recipe my friend, Jana Webb, shared with me. It is one of her family's favorites and is a great dish to take to a potluck.

2 ½ cups chopped fresh broccoli
½ cup raisins
¼ cup sunflower seeds (unsalted)
2 Tbl. diced red onion
2 Tbl. bacon-flavor soy bits
2 Tbl. nonfat plain yogurt
2 Tbl. light mayonnaise
1 ½ Tbl. sugar (or the equivalent in artificial sweetener)
½ Tbl. vinegar

Combine broccoli, raisins, sunflower seeds, onion and soy bits. Mix remaining ingredients together and add to broccoli mixture. Toss well to coat. Chill 2 hours or longer for flavors to blend.

Yield: 3 cups (6 servings)
One serving: ½ cup
Per serving: 132 calories, 17 grams carbohydrate, 4 grams protein, 5 grams fat
Exchanges: ½ starch, ½ medium-fat meat, ½ fruit, ½ fat

Hot German Potato Salad

The vinegar adds a special tang to this potato salad. Serve with low-fat franks or low-fat Polish turkey sausage.

1 lb. potatoes (about 4 cups, cubed)
³/₄ cup chopped onion
¹/₂ tsp. celery seeds
¹/₄ tsp. salt (optional)
¹/₈ tsp. pepper
³/₄ cup water
2 Tbl. unbleached flour
¹/₃ cup cider vinegar
1 Tbl. sugar (or the equivalent in artificial sweetener)
¹/₄ cup bacon-flavor soy bits

Scrub potatoes and cube. Place in medium saucepan and cover with water. Bring to a boil. Cover, reduce heat and simmer 12 minutes or until potatoes are done. Drain.

Spray a skillet with non-stick cooking spray. Sauté onions until done. Add celery seed, salt (optional), pepper, and water. Simmer on low. In a covered container, shake flour with vinegar to prevent lumps. Add to onions and cook, stirring constantly, until bubbly and thickened. Add sugar or artificial sweetener and stir. Carefully stir in potatoes. Serve hot, sprinkled with bacon bits.

Yield: 4 cups (8 servings)
One serving: ¹/₂ cup
Per serving: 100 calories, 20 grams carbohydrate, 3 grams protein, 1 gram fat
Exchanges: 1 starch

Mozzarella and Tomato Salad

Fresh tomatoes and deli-sliced mozzarella cheese make this a special dish. Have the tomatoes and cheese at room temperature for maximum flavor.

2 oz. part-skim mozzarella cheese, cut into very thin slices
2 medium tomatoes, cut in ¹/₄″ slices
1 Tbl. red wine vinegar
1 tsp. olive oil
¹/₂ tsp. Dijon mustard
¹/₂ tsp. dried parsley
¹/₄ tsp. dried basil
¹/₄ tsp. sugar (or the equivalent in artificial sweetener)
¹/₈ tsp. pepper

Cut sliced cheese into pieces that are about half the size of the tomato slices. On a large plate, alternate slices of tomato and mozzarella cheese. Arrange slices so that the top half of each tomato is not covered with cheese. Mix remaining ingredients and drizzle over salad just before serving. Serve at room temperature.

Yield: 4 servings
One serving: ¹/₄ recipe
Per serving: 72 calories, 5 grams carbohydrate, 4 grams protein, 4 grams fat
Exchanges: ¹/₂ medium-fat meat, 1 vegetable

Summer Cole Slaw

This simple recipe is popular at potlucks, but you may want to double the ingredients to serve a large crowd. Use a food processor for the cabbage to save time.

3 Tbl. light mayonnaise
3 Tbl. nonfat plain yogurt
2 tsp. cider vinegar
1 Tbl. sugar (or the equivalent in artificial sweetener)
¼ tsp. paprika
⅛ tsp. pepper
⅛ tsp. salt (optional)
5 cups finely shredded cabbage (about 1 ½ lbs.)

Make the dressing by mixing the mayonnaise, yogurt, vinegar, sugar, paprika, pepper and salt (optional). Add to the cabbage and stir until well combined.

Yield: 4 cups (8 servings)
One serving: ½ cup
Per serving: 43 calories, 6 grams carbohydrate, 1 gram protein, 2 grams fat
Exchanges: 1 vegetable, ½ fat

Variation: Add shredded carrots for color. For additional flavor, add diced onion and diced green pepper.

Vegetable Pasta Salad

You can substitute your favorite nonfat dressing in this recipe or use one that we've listed. This recipe also works well with other vegetables such as zucchini and tomatoes.

8 oz. rotini pasta - corkscrew shape (about 3 cups dry)
³/₄ cup broccoli flowerets
³/₄ cup cauliflower flowerets
³/₄ cup sliced cucumber
³/₄ cup sliced carrots
¹/₂ cup nonfat Italian or ranch-style dressing

Cook pasta according to package directions, omitting salt and oil. Drain and cool. Add vegetables and toss with dressing. Chill.

Yield: 7 cups (7 servings)
One serving: 1 cup
Per serving: 146 calories, 30 grams carbohydrate, 5 grams protein, 1 gram fat
Exchanges: 1 ¹/₂ starch, 1 vegetable

Confetti Salad

The eye appeal of this salad and the crunchy texture is a welcome change from traditional lettuce salads.

2 cups cooked brown rice (use quick-cooking)
1 can (17 oz.) whole kernel corn, drained*
1/2 cup diced green bell pepper
1/2 cup diced red bell pepper
4 green onions, chopped
1 tsp. dried thyme
1/3 cup nonfat Italian dressing

Combine all except the last ingredient. Pour dressing over mixture and toss well.

Yield: 5 cups (5 servings)
One serving: 1 cup
Per serving: 128 calories, 27 grams carbohydrate, 3 grams protein, 1 gram fat
Exchanges: 1 1/2 starch

Variation: Confetti Shrimp Salad - Add 1 lb. cooked shrimp and mix with vegetables before tossing with dressing.
Per serving: 213 calories, 27 grams carbohydrate, 22 grams protein, 2 grams fat
Exchanges**: 1 1/2 starch, 2 1/2 lean meat

*Sodium is figured for salt-free.

**Due to the low fat content of shrimp, calories are less than the exchanges would compute.

Bean and Pasta Salad

Serve this as a side dish or as a main dish salad. Either nonfat Italian or ranch-style dressing tastes good in this but you can also substitute your favorite nonfat dressing.

8 oz. rotini noodles - corkscrew shape (about 3 cups dry)
½ cup chopped green onion
1 can (15 ¼ oz.) kidney beans, drained*
1 ½ cups broccoli pieces
2 oz. grated reduced-fat cheddar cheese
6 Tbl. nonfat Italian or ranch-style dressing
1 tomato, chopped

Cook noodles according to package directions, omitting salt and oil. Drain and cool. In a large bowl, mix noodles, onion, kidney beans, broccoli and cheese. Toss with the dressing. Chill until serving. Toss with tomato just before serving.

Yield: 8 cups (8 servings)
One serving: 1 cup
Per serving: 188 calories, 33 grams carbohydrate, 9 grams protein, 2 grams fat
Exchanges: 2 starch, ½ lean meat, ½ vegetable

*Sodium is figured for salt-free.

Black Bean Salad

Serve this salad as a main dish or as a side dish. Remember this recipe when planning for a potluck.

1 can (15 oz.) black beans, drained and rinsed
1 can (17 oz.) whole kernel corn, drained*
1 cup diced red bell pepper
4 green onions, chopped
¼ tsp. onion powder
¼ tsp. dried oregano
⅛ tsp. garlic powder
⅛ tsp. cayenne pepper
½ cup nonfat Italian dressing

Combine all except the last ingredient. Pour dressing over mixture and toss well.

Yield: 4 cups (8 servings)
One serving: ½ cup
Per serving: 81 calories, 16 grams carbohydrate, 3 grams protein, 0 grams fat
Exchanges: 1 starch

*Sodium is figured for salt-free.

Beef, Bean and Pasta Salad

Add a fresh roll and you have a complete meal on a hot summer day. Keep this colorful dish in mind for potlucks.

6 oz. rotini noodles - corkscrew shape (about 2 cups dry)
½ lb. extra lean ground beef (9% fat) or ground turkey (7% fat)
½ cup nonfat ranch-style dressing
2-4 drops of Tabasco sauce
½ cup chopped green onion
1 can (15 ¼ oz.) kidney beans, drained*
4 oz. grated reduced-fat cheddar cheese
4 tomatoes, chopped

Cook noodles according to package directions, omitting salt and oil. Drain and cool. Cook meat in a skillet that has been sprayed with non-stick cooking spray. Set aside. Mix dressing and hot sauce. Add more Tabasco if you like a hot taste. Set aside. In a large bowl, mix noodles, meat, onion, kidney beans and cheese . Toss with the dressing. Chill until serving. Toss with tomatoes just before serving.

Yield: 9 cups (6 servings)
One serving: 1 ½ cups
Per serving: 342 calories, 43 grams carbohydrate, 22 grams protein, 9 grams fat
Exchanges: 2 ½ starch, 1 ½ medium-fat meat, 1 vegetable

*Sodium is figured for salt-free.

Taco Salad

Served on a bed of baked tortilla chips, this salad is a family favorite. If you like things on the spicy side, add 2 drops of Tabasco to the dressing.

$^1/_2$ lb. extra lean ground beef (9% fat) or ground turkey (7% fat)
$^1/_8$ tsp. chili powder
$^1/_8$ tsp. garlic powder
$^1/_8$ tsp. salt (optional)
$^1/_2$ head of lettuce, chopped
$^1/_2$ cup chopped green onion
3 tomatoes, chopped
1 can (15 $^1/_4$ oz.) kidney beans, drained*
4 oz. grated reduced-fat cheddar cheese
3 oz. tortilla chips, baked type**
$^3/_4$ cup nonfat thousand island or ranch-style dressing

Cook meat with the seasonings in a skillet that has been sprayed with non-stick cooking spray. Remove from heat. In a large bowl mix lettuce, onion, tomatoes, kidney beans, cheese, and meat. Divide tortilla chips on five individual plates and top with salad. Top with dressing and serve immediately.

Yield: 10 cups plus tortilla chips (5 servings)
One serving: 2 cups and 10 tortilla chips
Per serving: 323 calories, 34 grams carbohydrate, 23 grams protein, 11 grams fat
Exchanges: 2 starch, 2 medium-fat meat, 1 vegetable

*Sodium is figured for salt-free.

**Sodium is figured for salted. People on low-sodium diets should use the unsalted variety of baked tortilla chips.

Chicken Caesar Salad

For that hot summer evening, serve this simple salad with French bread or a hard roll.

4 skinless, boneless chicken breasts (about 1 lb.)
1 ½ quarts Romaine lettuce
½ red onion, sliced thin
¼ cup nonfat Italian dressing or light Caesar dressing
4 tsp. grated Parmesan cheese

Cook chicken breasts by one of the following methods:

Microwave Oven: Arrange on a microwave-safe baking dish in a circle on the outer portion of the dish. Cover with wax paper and microwave on high for 5 minutes, rearranging halfway through cooking time. Let sit a few minutes before cutting into strips.

Stove Top: Place chicken in a pan and cover with water. Cover and simmer on low until tender (about 15-20 minutes). Drain liquid and save for soups.

Meanwhile, arrange salad greens on 4 plates. Cut each chicken breast in one-inch strips. Arrange chicken and onion on salad greens. Drizzle 1 tablespoon of salad dressing over each salad. Sprinkle with Parmesan cheese.

Yield: 4 servings
One serving: ¼ recipe
Per serving: 168 calories, 6 grams carbohydrate, 28 grams protein, 4 grams fat
Exchanges*: 3 ½ lean meat, 1 vegetable

*Due to the low fat content of chicken breasts, calories are less than the exchanges would compute.

Chicken Rainbow Salad

This is a very good main dish salad for the summertime or it can be served as a side salad anytime. For an attractive presentation, serve each portion on a bed of Romaine lettuce.

8 oz. tricolored rotini noodles - corkscrew shape (about 3 cups dry)
2 cups cooked, cubed chicken
1 medium cucumber, sliced
1 cup sliced celery
½ red onion, sliced thin
½ cup light mayonnaise
¼ cup light sour cream
2 Tbl. skim milk
1 tsp. dried dill weed
1 tsp. salt (optional)
¼ tsp. pepper

Cook pasta according to package directions, omitting salt and oil. Drain. Meanwhile, in a large bowl, combine chicken, cucumber, celery and onion. Mix in pasta. In small bowl, blend mayonnaise, sour cream, milk and seasonings. Toss dressing with salad mixture.

Yield: 8 cups (6 servings)
One serving: 1 ¼ cups
Per serving: 302 calories, 34 grams carbohydrate, 21 grams protein, 9 grams fat
Exchanges: 2 starch, 2 lean meat, 1 fat

Variation: Rainbow Vegetable Salad - Omit chicken and reduce the mayonnaise to ⅓ cup. Serve as a side dish.
Per serving: 200 calories, 33 grams carbohydrate, 6 grams protein, 5 grams fat
Exchanges: 2 starch, 1 fat

Hawaiian Chicken Salad

This delicious salad is a complete meal. My friend, Yvonne Lorenz, shared this recipe with me, and it is a great recipe for using leftover turkey.

2 cups cooked chicken or turkey, cubed
2 cups cold cooked brown rice (use quick-cooking)
1 cup celery, diced
1 can (8 oz.) sliced water chestnuts, drained
1 can (15 ¼ oz.) pineapple tidbits, drained
⅓ cup light mayonnaise
2 Tbl. skim milk
1 Tbl. lemon juice
½ tsp. salt (optional)
½ tsp. curry
¼ tsp. pepper

In a large bowl, mix chicken, rice, celery, water chestnuts and pineapple. In a smaller bowl, mix the remaining ingredients for the dressing. Toss dressing with the chicken mixture.

Yield: about 6 cups (4 servings)
One serving: 1 ½ cups
Per serving: 294 calories, 28 grams carbohydrate, 24 grams protein, 9 grams fat
Exchanges: 1 ½ starch, 3 lean meat, ½ fruit

Turkey Rotini Salad

This main dish salad can be served as is or on a bed of lettuce. You can use leftover turkey or chicken in this recipe.

4 oz. rotini noodles - corkscrew shape (about 1 ½ cups dry)
¾ cup broccoli flowerets
¾ cup sliced carrots
1 ½ cups cooked cubed turkey breast
3 Tbl. nonfat Italian or ranch-style dressing

Cook pasta according to package directions, omitting salt and oil. Drain and cool. Add vegetables and turkey. Toss with dressing.

Yield: 5 cups (5 servings)
One serving: 1 cup
Per serving: 169 calories, 22 grams carbohydrate, 16 grams protein, 2 grams fat
Exchanges: 1 starch, 1 ½ meat, ½ vegetable

Seafood Pasta Salad

Here is a salad that is colorful, easy to prepare, and one that the whole family will enjoy. Either cooked shrimp or fresh crab can be used in place of imitation crab.

4 oz. rotini noodles - corkscrew shape (about 1 ½ cups dry)
8 oz. imitation crabmeat
4 oz. grated reduced-fat cheddar cheese
1 cup chopped celery
½ cup chopped red bell pepper
3-4 green onions, chopped
½ cup nonfat ranch-style dressing

Prepare noodles according to package directions, omitting salt and oil. Drain and set aside. In a large bowl, mix together crabmeat, cheese, celery, bell pepper and onion. Toss with noodles and dressing. Refrigerate to chill thoroughly before serving.

Yield: 7 cups (7 servings)
One serving: 1 cup
Per serving: 157 calories, 19 grams carbohydrate, 13 grams protein, 3 grams fat
Exchanges: 1 starch, 1 ½ lean meat

Tuna Macaroni Salad

Try this on a hot summer evening served on a bed of lettuce accompanied with sliced tomatoes. A whole wheat roll completes this meal.

4 oz. medium-size sea shell pasta (about 2 cups dry)
1 cup chopped celery
1 cup chopped red bell pepper
½ cup sliced green onion
2 cans (6 ⅛ oz. each) water pack tuna, drained
½ cup nonfat ranch-style dressing

Cook macaroni according to package directions, omitting salt and oil. Drain. Add remaining ingredients and toss with dressing. Refrigerate until serving.

Yield: 6 cups (6 servings)
One serving: 1 cup
Per serving: 151 calories, 19 grams carbohydrate, 16 grams protein, 1 gram fat
Exchanges*: 1 starch, 2 lean meat, ½ vegetable

*Due to the low fat content of tuna fish, calories are less than the exchanges would compute.

Rice, Bean and Pasta Side Dishes

Many of the recipes in this section not only work well as a side dish, but can also be served in a larger portion for a main dish. The bean dishes are my favorite. A variety of pasta shapes are used throughout this book, but you can easily substitute with any pasta you have on hand.

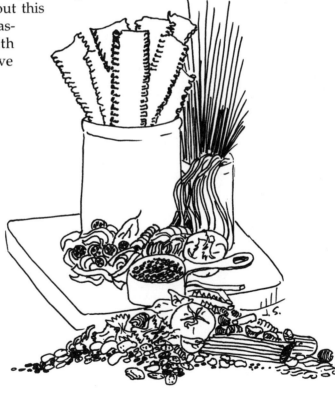

Creamy Dill Fettucini

This is a quick side dish that will dress up any meal. Double this recipe to serve as a main dish.

6 oz. fettucini noodles, dry
3 Tbl. unbleached flour
1 ½ cups skim milk, divided
2 tsp. dried dill weed
¼ tsp. salt (optional)
⅛ tsp. pepper
3 oz. reduced-fat sharp cheddar cheese, cut in small pieces

Prepare noodles according to package instructions, omitting oil and salt. Meanwhile, prepare the sauce by combining the flour with ½ cup of milk in a covered container and shake well to prevent lumps. Pour into a 4-cup glass measuring cup along with the remainder of the milk and seasonings.

Cook in the microwave on high for 4-5 minutes, or until thickened, stirring with a wire whisk every 60 seconds to prevent lumping. Add cheese and stir until melted. Toss with noodles before serving.

Yield: 3 cups (6 servings)
One serving: ½ cup
Per serving: 183 calories, 28 grams carbohydrate, 11 grams protein, 3 grams fat
Exchanges: 2 starch, ½ medium-fat meat

Dijon Fettucini

These rich-tasting noodles are a good side dish with chicken, pork, seafood or beef.

$1/4$ cup light mayonnaise
$1/4$ cup nonfat plain yogurt
2 tsp. Dijon mustard
2 tsp. dried parsley
2 tsp. chopped garlic
6 oz. fettucini noodles, dry

Mix mayonnaise, yogurt, mustard, parsley and garlic to make the sauce. Set aside. Meanwhile, cook the fettucini according to package directions, omitting oil and salt. Drain. Add the sauce to the noodles and toss. Cook on low until heated throughout.

Yield: 3 cups (6 servings)
One serving: $1/2$ cup
Per serving: 144 calories, 24 grams carbohydrate, 4 grams protein, 4 grams fat
Exchanges: $1 1/2$ starch, $1/2$ fat

Szechuan Pasta

This spicy-hot dish is a good accompaniment to any meat or seafood. You can make this into a complete meal by adding leftover poultry or meat to the sauce.

8 oz. egg noodles - "no yolk" type (4 cups dry)
½ cup chicken broth, fat removed*
1 ½ tsp. cornstarch
2 cups sliced vegetables (green bell pepper, broccoli, pea pods, etc.)
1-2 Tbl. Szechuan sauce
¼ cup dry roasted peanuts, unsalted

Prepare noodles according to package directions, omitting salt and oil. Drain. Spray skillet with non-stick cooking spray. In a covered container, shake chicken broth and cornstarch. Add to skillet with vegetables. Cook until bubbly and thickened, stirring constantly. Add Szechuan sauce and peanuts. Toss noodles with the sauce.

Yield: 6 cups (8 servings)
One serving: ¾ cup
Per serving: 147 calories, 25 grams carbohydrate, 6 grams protein, 3 grams fat
Exchanges: 1 ½ starch, ½ vegetable, ½ fat

*Sodium is figured for salt-free.

Seasoned Black Beans

Most of the canned black beans are not seasoned and need a little perking up before serving. This recipe makes a good side dish.

1 can (15 oz.) black beans, drained and rinsed
¼ tsp. onion powder
¼ tsp. dried oregano
⅛ tsp. cayenne pepper
⅛ tsp. garlic powder

Mix all ingredients in a microwave-safe dish. Cover and heat in microwave on high about 1 minute, stirring halfway through cooking time.

Yield: 3 servings (1 cup)
One serving: ⅓ cup
Per serving: 103 calories, 18 grams carbohydrate, 7 grams protein, 0 grams fat
Exchanges: 1 starch

Spanish Rice and Beans

This is a colorful side dish that tastes great with the Spanish Chicken found on page 178. For a different flavor, try substituting black beans for the kidney beans.

1 cup quick-cooking brown rice, uncooked
$1/8$ tsp. cumin
1 $1/4$ cups chicken broth, fat removed*
1 can (15 $1/4$ oz.) kidney beans, drained*
1 can (4 oz.) diced green chiles

Cook rice according to package directions adding the cumin, substituting chicken broth for water and omitting the salt. When done, mix in remaining ingredients and cover to heat thoroughly.

Yield: 4 cups (8 servings)
One serving: $1/2$ cup
Per serving: 85 calories, 16 grams carbohydrate, 4 grams protein, 0 grams fat
Exchanges: 1 starch

*Sodium is figured for salt-free.

Spicy Spanish Rice

Serve this recipe as a side dish with Mexican food. The green pepper and tomato add color as well as vitamins and minerals to this dish.

¹/₃ **cup salsa, thick and chunky**
1 cup water
1 green bell pepper, finely diced
1 can (16 oz.) diced tomatoes, not drained*
1 ¹/₂ cups quick-cooking brown rice, uncooked
¹/₄ **tsp. dried thyme**
¹/₄ **tsp. salt (optional)**
¹/₈ **tsp. pepper**

Spray a large skillet with non-stick cooking spray. Add all ingredients and mix well. Bring to a boil. Reduce heat to low. Cover and simmer 25 minutes or until most of the liquid is absorbed, stirring occasionally.

Yield: 5 cups (5 servings)
One serving: 1 cup
Per serving: 131 calories, 27 grams carbohydrate, 3 grams protein, 1 gram fat
Exchanges: 1 ¹/₂ starch, 1 vegetable

*Sodium is figured for salt-free.

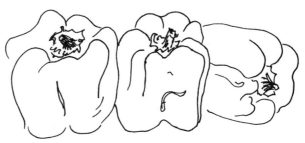

$\mathcal{S}$andwiches

Using different breads and fillings adds variety to traditional sandwiches.
I especially like the recipes that use several vegetables.

Black Bean Quesadillas

This recipe may be used as part of a meal or the quesadillas can be cut in wedges for an appetizer. The microwave makes this especially quick.

1 can (15 oz.) black beans, drained and rinsed
2 Tbl. salsa, thick and chunky
¹/₄ tsp. onion powder
¹/₄ tsp. dried oregano
¹/₈ tsp. cayenne pepper
¹/₈ tsp. garlic powder
2 Tbl. chopped green onion
4 flour tortillas (7 ¹/₂″ diameter)
2 oz. grated reduced-fat cheddar cheese

Mash beans. Add salsa, seasonings and onion. Mix well.

Microwave Oven: Spoon filling onto half of each tortilla. Top with cheese and fold each tortilla in half. Microwave on high for 60 seconds, rotating ¹/₄ turn halfway through cooking time.

Skillet or Griddle: Divide filling onto 2 tortillas. Top with cheese and the remaining two tortillas. Spray griddle or skillet with non-stick cooking spray and brown quesadillas on both sides. Cut in half or quarters before serving.

Yield: 4 servings
One serving: ¹/₄ recipe
Per serving: 234 calories, 34 grams carbohydrate, 12 grams protein, 5 grams fat
Exchanges: 2 starch, 1 medium-fat meat

Cheese and Chile Quesadillas

Serve these for a light meal when you really don't think you have time to make dinner. Add fresh sliced fruit for a side dish. These also make a good appetizer.

¼ cup diced green chiles
4 flour tortillas (7 ½" diameter)
4 oz. grated reduced-fat cheddar cheese

Microwave Oven: Divide chiles onto half of each tortilla. Top with cheese and fold each tortilla in half. Microwave on high for 60 seconds, rotating ¼ turn halfway through cooking time.

Skillet or Griddle: Divide chiles onto 2 tortillas. Top with cheese and the remaining two tortillas. Spray griddle or skillet with non-stick cooking spray and brown quesadillas on both sides. Cut in half or quarters before serving.

Yield: 4 servings
One serving: ¼ recipe
Per serving: 203 calories, 21 grams carbohydrate, 12 grams protein, 8 grams fat
Exchanges: 1 ½ starch, 1 medium-fat meat

Tuna Quesadillas

Serve this as an appetizer or for a light meal. This is a favorite for kids and adults alike.

1 can (6 ⅛ oz.) water packed tuna, drained
1 Tbl. light mayonnaise or salad dressing
4 flour tortillas (7 ½" diameter)
2 oz. grated reduced-fat cheddar cheese

Flake tuna with a fork if it is in chunks. Combine with mayonnaise.

Microwave Oven: Spoon filling onto half of each tortilla. Top with cheese and fold each tortilla in half. Microwave on high for 60 seconds, rotating ¼ turn halfway through cooking time.

Skillet or Griddle: Divide filling onto 2 tortillas. Top with cheese and the remaining two tortillas. Spray griddle or skillet with non-stick cooking spray and brown quesadillas on both sides. Cut in half or quarters before serving.

Yield: 4 servings
One serving: ¼ recipe
Per serving: 213 calories, 20 grams carbohydrate, 18 grams protein, 6 grams fat
Exchanges: 1 ½ starch, 2 lean meat

Tuna Burgers

A great low-fat substitute for the all-American hamburger. It makes a good sandwich or a light evening meal.

1 can (6-7 oz. each) tuna packed in water, drained
2 Tbl. light mayonnaise
1 Tbl. pickle relish
1 tsp. lemon juice
1 tsp. dried parsley
½ tsp. onion powder
2 drops Tabasco sauce
3 saltines (unsalted top), crushed
2 hamburger buns

Optional toppings:
 nonfat tartar sauce or salad dressing
 tomato & onion slices
 lettuce

Flake tuna and mix with remaining ingredients, except buns. Form into 2 patties and proceed with one of the methods below.

Conventional Oven: Preheat oven to 350 degrees. Arrange patties on a baking sheet that has been sprayed with non-stick cooking spray. Bake for 25 minutes or until golden brown.

Stove Top: Spray a griddle or large skillet with non-stick cooking spray. Cook each patty a few minutes on each side until golden brown.

Heat buns in oven or microwave until warm. Serve patties on hamburger buns topped with optional ingredients.

Yield: 2 servings
One serving: 1 patty and 1 bun
Per serving: 293 calories, 29 grams carbohydrate, 26 grams protein, 8 grams fat
Exchanges: 2 starch, 3 lean meat

Variation: Serve tuna patties with Creamy Mashed Potatoes, on page 90, and a vegetable.

Broiled Seafood Muffins

This recipe is a good choice for a luncheon or light supper. Tuna can be substituted for the seafood listed.

2 English muffins, split
2 Tbl. light mayonnaise or salad dressing
4 oz. cooked crab, shrimp, or fish
2 oz. grated reduced-fat cheddar cheese

Toast muffins. Spread with mayonnaise. Top with seafood and cheese. Broil until cheese melts.

Yield: 4 halves (2 servings)
One serving: 2 halves
Per serving: 290 calories, 28 grams carbohydrate, 26 grams protein, 8 grams fat
Exchanges: 2 starch, 2 ^{1}/$_2$ lean meat

Ricotta Pizza

If you like pizza but want to find a low-fat version, try this one. The Ricotta cheese adds a delicate flavor to the pizza.

1 (16 oz.) Boboli Italian Bread Shell
^{1}/$_4$ cup pizza sauce
1 cup low-fat Ricotta cheese
^{1}/$_2$ green bell pepper, sliced thin
^{1}/$_2$ small onion, sliced thin
1 medium tomato, sliced thin

Preheat oven to 450 degrees. Place Boboli on pizza pan and spread pizza sauce over surface. Spread Ricotta cheese over sauce and top with peppers and onions. Bake for 8-10 minutes. Arrange tomato slices over pizza.

Yield: 8 slices (8 servings)
One serving: 1 slice
Per serving: 173 calories, 25 grams carbohydrate, 9 grams protein, 4 grams fat
Exchanges: 1 ^{1}/$_2$ starch, ^{1}/$_2$ medium-fat meat, ^{1}/$_2$ vegetable

Chili Dogs

Reduced-fat products help to make this a good low-fat choice. Children really like this. However, anyone on a sodium restricted diet needs to be cautious as it is still high in sodium.

6 reduced-fat hot dogs (less than 1.5 g of fat each)
1 can (15 oz.) reduced-fat turkey chili with beans*
6 hot dog buns

Optional toppings:
6 Tbl. chopped onion
3 oz. grated reduced-fat cheddar cheese

Place hot dogs in a saucepan and cover with water. Cover and bring to a boil. Remove from heat and let sit for 10 minutes. Meanwhile, heat chili in the microwave or on the stove top until hot. Wrap buns in a napkin and heat in the microwave on high for 25 to 35 seconds until warm. To serve, fill each bun with one hot dog, 1/4 cup chili, and pass the optional toppings.

Yield: 6 chili dogs (6 servings)
One serving: 1 chili dog
Per serving: 249 calories, 34 grams carbohydrate, 17 grams protein, 5 grams fat
Exchanges: 2 starch, 1 1/2 lean meat

*or choose another chili with no more than 8 grams of fat per 220 calories.

Beef and Cabbage Sandwich

This is a complete meal in a pocket. Try this recipe on one of those hurried evenings.

½ lb. top sirloin steak, cut in bite-size pieces
1 onion, sliced
2 cups shredded cabbage
⅛ tsp. salt (optional)
dash pepper
1 tsp. caraway seeds
1 tsp. dried parsley
2 whole wheat Pita breads
½ cup nonfat plain yogurt
2 tsp. Dijon mustard

Spray a skillet with non-stick cooking spray. Brown the steak and onion. Add cabbage, salt (optional), pepper, caraway and parsley. Continue to stir-fry until vegetables and meat are tender. Cut Pita bread in half and microwave on high for 20 seconds or until warm. Meanwhile, mix yogurt with mustard. Spread 2 Tbl. of yogurt mixture in each Pita bread half. Fill with beef stir-fry.

Yield: 4 half sandwiches (4 servings)
One serving: 1 half sandwich
Per serving: 201 calories, 25 grams carbohydrate, 17 grams protein, 4 grams fat
Exchanges: 1 ½ starch, 1 ½ lean meat, 1 vegetable

Chicken Stir-Fry Sandwich

This sandwich is a good choice for lunch or a light supper. Substitute fresh vegetables in season. Zucchini works well.

¹/₂ lb. boneless, skinless chicken breasts, cut in strips
¹/₂ red bell pepper, sliced
¹/₂ green bell pepper, sliced
¹/₄ cup chopped green onion
1 tsp. chopped garlic
1 tsp. dried parsley
¹/₄ tsp. dried thyme
¹/₈ tsp. salt (optional)
¹/₁₆ tsp. pepper
2 whole wheat Pita breads
¹/₄ cup nonfat plain yogurt or nonfat ranch-style dressing

Spray a skillet with non-stick cooking spray. Add chicken, vegetables and seasonings. Stir-fry until chicken is done and vegetables are to your liking. Cut Pita bread in half and microwave on high for 20 seconds or until warm. Spread 1 Tbl. of yogurt or dressing in each Pita bread half. Fill with chicken stir-fry.

Yield: 4 half sandwiches (4 servings)
One serving: 1 half sandwich
Per serving: 170 calories, 20 grams carbohydrate, 17 grams protein, 2 grams fat
Exchanges*: 1 ¹/₂ starch, 2 lean meat

*Due to the low fat content of chicken breasts, calories are less than the exchanges would compute.

Turkey Reuben Sandwich

This is a low-fat version of a high-fat sandwich. Use of low-fat ingredients and the elimination of margarine makes this tasty and yet healthy. If you are on a sodium restricted diet, rinsing the sauerkraut helps to reduce the sodium but it does not eliminate it.

8 slices of rye bread
4 oz. sliced turkey
1 cup sauerkraut, rinsed well and drained
4 oz. sliced low-fat Swiss cheese

Preheat to 400 degrees. Toast bread. On each of 4 slices, place 1 oz. turkey, 1/4 cup sauerkraut and 1 oz. Swiss cheese. Top with remaining slices of bread. Wrap in aluminum foil and bake for 10 minutes or until thoroughly heated and cheese is melted.

Yield: 4 sandwiches (4 servings)
One serving: 1 sandwich
Per serving: 311 calories, 34 grams carbohydrate, 24 grams protein, 8 grams fat
Exchanges: 2 starch, 1 lean meat, 1 medium-fat meat, 1/2 vegetable

Garden Deli Sandwich

This is a simple sandwich and a good way to use cucumbers and tomatoes from the garden. Zucchini can be substituted for the cucumbers.

4 Tbl. light cream cheese
1 whole wheat Pita bread
8 cucumber slices
4 tomato slices
1 cup alfalfa sprouts

Cut Pita bread in half. Spread cream cheese inside Pita bread. Add sliced vegetables and sprouts.

Yield: 2 half sandwiches (1 serving)
One serving: 2 halves
Per serving: 347 calories, 45 grams carbohydrate, 14 grams protein, 12 grams fat
Exchanges: $1/2$ milk, 2 $1/2$ starch, 1 vegetable, 2 fat

Vegetable Pita Sandwich

This sandwich is good hot or cold. We did not use a dressing as we felt there was enough moisture from the tomatoes and the cucumbers.

8 cucumber slices
4 tomato slices
4 bell pepper slices (red or green)
1 oz. sliced reduced-fat cheddar cheese
1 whole wheat Pita bread

Cut Pita bread in half. Divide sliced vegetables and cheese inside each half. Serve cold or heat in microwave on high for 50 seconds, rotating $1/4$ turn halfway through cooking time, or until cheese is melted.

Yield: 2 halves (1 serving)
One serving: 2 halves
Per serving: 305 calories, 43 grams carbohydrate, 17 grams protein, 7 grams fat
Exchanges: 2 $1/2$ starch, 1 medium-fat meat, 1 vegetable

Vegetable Stir-Fry Sandwich

This sandwich is a good choice for a luncheon or a light supper. Feel free to vary the vegetables to whatever is in season.

1 small zucchini, sliced
1 red pepper, sliced
1 medium onion, sliced
$^1/_2$ tsp. dried parsley
$^1/_8$ tsp. dried thyme
$^1/_8$ tsp. salt (optional)
dash pepper
2 whole wheat Pita breads
$^1/_2$ cup light cream cheese

Spray a skillet with non-stick cooking spray. Add vegetables and seasonings. Stir-fry until vegetables are cooked to your liking. Cut Pita bread in half and microwave on high for 20 seconds or until warm. Spread 2 Tbl. of cream cheese in each Pita bread half. Fill with stir-fried vegetables.

Yield: 4 half sandwiches (4 servings)
One serving: 1 half sandwich
Per serving: 190 calories, 26 grams carbohydrate, 7 grams protein, 6 grams fat
Exchanges: 1 $^1/_2$ starch, 1 vegetable, 1 fat

Meatless Entrees

You don't have to be a vegetarian to appreciate the good-tasting recipes in this section. My family's favorites are the Eggplant Parmesan and the Rice and Bean Burritos. Both are easy enough for kids to prepare.

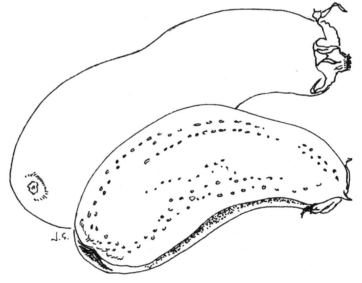

Broccoli Quiche

This is a great choice for a women's brunch or luncheon. Serve with a fruit cup or orange wedges.

3 flour tortillas (7 ½" diameter)
2 cups broccoli pieces
½ cup sliced green onion
4 oz. grated reduced-fat cheddar cheese
2 cups egg substitute (equal to 8 eggs)
¼ cup skim milk
¼ tsp. paprika
8 tomato slices

Preheat oven to 350 degrees. Spray a 9" pie pan with non-stick cooking spray. Cut 2 tortillas in half and place each half in the pan so that the rounded edge is ¼ inch above the rim. Place the remaining tortilla in the center of the pan. Add broccoli, onion and cheese. Mix eggs with milk and pour over top. Sprinkle with paprika.

Bake for 45 minutes or until a knife inserted in the center comes out clean. Let sit for 10 minutes before cutting into 8 wedges. Top each piece with a tomato slice.

Yield: 8 servings
One serving: ⅛ recipe
Per serving: 129 calories, 12 grams carbohydrate, 12 grams protein, 4 grams fat
Exchanges: ½ starch, 1 medium-fat meat, 1 vegetable

Sausage Quiche

This appealing dish is assembled in minutes. It's great for a brunch or breakfast served with fresh fruit. Because of the higher sodium content of sausage links, it should be limited by those on low-sodium diets.

3 flour tortillas (7 ½″ diameter)
8 vegetarian sausage links
2 oz. grated reduced-fat cheddar cheese
1 can (4 oz.) sliced mushrooms, drained and rinsed
2 ½ cups egg substitute (equal to 10 eggs)
½ cup skim milk
½ Tbl. dried parsley
¼ tsp. paprika

Preheat oven to 350 degrees. Spray a 9″ pie pan with non-stick cooking spray. Cut 2 tortillas in half and place each half in the pan so that the rounded edge is ¼ inch above the rim. Place the remaining tortilla in the center of the pan. Place the sausage links over the tortillas in a spoke-like fashion. Top with cheese and mushrooms. Mix eggs with milk and pour over top. Sprinkle with parsley and paprika. Bake for 45-50 minutes or until a knife inserted in the center comes out clean. Let sit for 10 minutes before cutting into 8 wedges.

Yield: 8 servings
One serving: ⅛ recipe
Per serving: 152 calories, 12 grams carbohydrate, 15 grams protein, 5 grams fat
Exchanges: 1 starch, 1 ½ lean meat

Spanish Quiche

This is an easy supper or brunch dish that will be a favorite for anyone who likes Mexican food. Seasoned Black Beans on page 125 can be substituted for the refried beans. Pass the salsa!

3 flour tortillas (7 ½" diameter)
1 can (16 oz.) vegetarian refried beans
1 can (4 oz.) diced green chiles
½ cup sliced green onion
4 oz. grated reduced-fat cheddar cheese
1 ¾ cups egg substitute (equal to 7 eggs)
¼ cup skim milk
¼ tsp. paprika

Preheat oven to 350 degrees. Spray a 9" pie pan with non-stick cooking spray. Cut 2 tortillas in half and place each half in the pan so that the rounded edge is ¼ inch above the rim. Place the remaining tortilla in the center of the pan. Spread beans over tortillas. Top with chiles, onion and cheese. Mix eggs with milk and pour over top. Sprinkle with paprika.

Bake for 50 minutes or until a knife inserted in the center comes out clean. Let sit for 10 minutes before cutting into 8 wedges.

Yield: 8 servings
One serving: ⅛ recipe
Per serving: 175 calories, 19 grams carbohydrate, 14 grams protein, 5 grams fat
Exchanges: 1 ½ starch, 1 lean meat

Cheese and Tortilla Lasagna

The crunch of the corn adds an interesting texture to this dish. If you are serving a crowd, double this recipe and cook in a 9" x 13" pan.

1 can (16 oz.) diced tomatoes, not drained*
1 can (8 oz.) tomato sauce*
1 can (8 oz.) whole kernel corn, drained*
1 can (4 oz.) diced green chiles
1 tsp. chili powder
3/4 tsp. cumin
1/4 tsp. pepper
1/8 tsp. garlic powder
1/16 tsp. cayenne pepper
1/4 cup egg substitute (equal to 1 egg)
2 cups low-fat cottage cheese
7 corn tortillas, cut in strips
2 oz. grated reduced-fat cheddar cheese

Preheat oven to 350 degrees. Mix canned tomatoes with tomato sauce, corn, chiles and seasonings. Set aside. Mix egg substitute with cottage cheese and set aside. Spray an 8" x 8" pan with non-stick cooking spray. Layer in this order: 1/3 tortillas, 1/3 cheese mixture, 1/3 tomato mixture, repeat twice ending with tomato mixture.

Bake for 30 minutes or until bubbly. Sprinkle with grated cheese and return to oven until melted.

Yield: 6 servings
One serving: 1/6 recipe
Per serving: 220 calories, 28 grams carbohydrate, 18 grams protein, 4 grams fat
Exchanges: 1 1/2 starch, 1 1/2 meat, 1 vegetable

*Sodium is figured for salt-free.

Cheese and Noodle Bake

This is a healthy variation of macaroni and cheese that your family will enjoy.

8 oz. elbow macaroni (about 2 cups dry)
1 ½ cup skim milk, divided
3 Tbl. unbleached flour
¼ tsp. salt (optional)
⅛ tsp. pepper
3 oz. grated reduced-fat sharp cheddar cheese or 4 Tbl. grated Parmesan cheese
1 oz. grated reduced-fat sharp cheddar cheese

Prepare macaroni according to package directions, omitting salt and oil. Drain and set aside. Combine ½ cup milk with flour in covered container and shake well to prevent lumps. Pour flour mixture and the rest of the milk into a 2-quart covered glass casserole and cook in the microwave on high for 4-5 minutes, stirring every minute until bubbly and thickened. Mix in seasonings and all but 1 oz. of cheddar cheese. Add cooked noodles. Cover and cook on high for 3 minutes, rotating ¼ turn halfway through cooking. Stir. Sprinkle with cheddar cheese. Cover and let sit 10 minutes before serving.

Yield: about 5 cups (4 servings)
One serving: ¼ recipe
Per serving: 345 calories, 52 grams carbohydrate, 20 grams protein, 6 grams fat
Exchanges: 3 ½ starch, 1 ½ medium-fat meat

Variation: Sausage and Noodle Bake - Add 8 oz. of chopped turkey smoked sausage (Polish kielbasa type, 90% fat-free) when adding the cooked noodles. Note: If you are on a low sodium diet, you should limit the use of this recipe because of the high sodium content of sausage.
Per serving: 430 calories, 54 grams carbohydrate, 30 grams protein, 10 grams fat
Exchanges: 3 ½ starch, 2 ½ lean meat

Eggplant Lasagna

You save time with this recipe because you don't precook the noodles. This is another good meatless meal that your whole family will enjoy. In the summertime, substitute 1 1/2 cups of fresh sliced vegetables (zucchini works well) for each layer of eggplant. If you are on a low-sodium diet, use low-salt cheeses in this recipe.

1 cup low-fat ricotta cheese
1 cup low-fat cottage cheese
2 Tbl. dried parsley
1 tsp. chopped garlic
5 cups spaghetti sauce (less than 4g fat per 4 oz.)
12 oz. lasagna noodles, dry
1 small eggplant (about 14 oz.), peeled and sliced thin
4 oz. grated part-skim mozzarella cheese
1/4 cup grated Parmesan cheese

Preheat oven to 350 degrees. Mix ricotta cheese, cottage cheese, parsley and garlic. Peel eggplant and slice about 1/4 inch thick. In a 9" x 13" pan that has been sprayed with a non-stick cooking spray, pour in 1 cup spaghetti sauce. Arrange 1/3 of the noodles in the pan so that they touch but do not overlap.

Layer in this order: half the eggplant, mozzarella cheese, 1 cup of sauce, 1/3 lasagna noodles, cheese mixture, remainder of the eggplant, 1 cup of spaghetti sauce, remainder of lasagna noodles and the remainder of the spaghetti sauce. Sprinkle with Parmesan cheese. Bake, covered tightly with aluminum foil, for one hour.

Yield: 8 servings
One serving: 1/8 of recipe
Per serving: 338 calories, 51 grams carbohydrate, 20 grams protein, 6 grams fat
Exchanges: 2 1/2 starch, 1 medium-fat meat, 3 vegetable

Eggplant Parmesan

Quick, easy and delicious! This dish is so quick to put together that it will be one that you make often. Serve with a side dish of pasta and a tossed salad.

2 ¹/₂ cups spaghetti sauce (less than 4g fat per 4 oz)
1 medium eggplant (about 1 ¹/₂ -2 lbs.)
4 oz. grated part-skim mozzarella cheese
grated Parmesan cheese (optional)

Preheat oven to 350 degrees. Spray a 9″ x 13″ pan with non-stick cooking spray. Pour ¹/₂ cup of sauce in pan. Peel eggplant and slice ¹/₂″ thick. Arrange half of the slices in the baking pan. Top with 1 cup of sauce, half of the mozzarella cheese, the remainder of the eggplant slices, and the remainder of the sauce.

Cover with aluminum foil and bake for 45-55 minutes. Top with remainder of mozzarella cheese and return to oven, uncovered, until cheese is melted. Serve with Parmesan cheese (optional).

Yield: 4 servings
One serving: ¹/₄ recipe
Per serving: 188 calories, 24 grams carbohydrate, 11 grams protein, 5 grams fat
Exchanges: 1 medium-fat meat, 4 vegetable

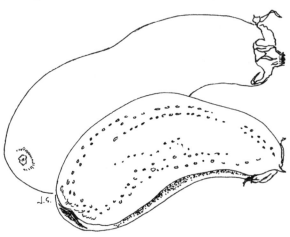

Harvest Primavera

This recipe takes advantage of fresh vegetables in season. Although this may not be a favorite with children, it is definitely popular with adults.

8 oz. egg noodles - "no yolk" type (4 cups dry)
1 cup chopped onion
1 cup sliced zucchini
1 cup sliced yellow summer squash
1 cup chopped bell pepper, red, green or yellow
2 cups spaghetti sauce (less than 4g fat per 4 oz.)
1 Tbl. grated Parmesan cheese

Cook noodles according to package directions, omitting salt and oil. Drain. Proceed with either stove top or microwave directions below.

Stove Top: Mix vegetables and spaghetti sauce in a saucepan and simmer until vegetables are tender, about 20-30 minutes. Spoon vegetable mixture over noodles and serve with Parmesan cheese.

Microwave Oven: Mix vegetables and spaghetti sauce in a covered 2-quart glass casserole and cook on high for 8 minutes, stirring halfway through cooking time. Spoon vegetable mixture over noodles and serve with Parmesan cheese.

Yield: 4 cups of sauce and 4 cups of noodles (5 servings)
One serving: ¾ cup of noodles and ¾ cup of sauce
Per serving: 241 calories, 47 grams carbohydrate, 9 grams protein, 2 grams fat
Exchanges: 2 ½ starch, 2 vegetable

Italian Curry Pasta

Served as a main dish or a side dish, the addition of curry with fresh tomatoes makes this dish a uniquely flavorful combination that will attract many compliments. If you are not especially fond of curry in foods, use the lesser amount and you will still like this recipe.

1 tsp. chopped garlic
1 onion, chopped
3 large tomatoes, chopped
1 tsp. cumin
1 or 2 tsp. curry
½ tsp. coriander
½ tsp. salt (optional)
6 oz. angel hair pasta, dry
2 Tbl. grated Parmesan cheese

Spray a skillet with non-stick cooking spray. Add vegetables and seasonings. Simmer for 15-20 minutes, or until thickened. Meanwhile, prepare pasta according to package directions, omitting salt and oil. Drain pasta. Pour sauce over pasta and toss. Serve sprinkled with Parmesan cheese.

Yield: 5 cups (4 servings)
One serving: 1 ¼ cups
Per serving: 260 calories, 49 grams carbohydrate, 10 grams protein, 3 grams fat
Exchanges: 2 starch, 3 ½ vegetable

Pesto Linguini

It doesn't get much easier than this. Serve as a main dish or as a side dish. This goes well with our Focaccia cheese bread. When using pesto sauce, limit the amount you use because it is high in fat and just a small amount provides a good flavor.

12 oz. linguini, dry
4 Tbl. pesto sauce
grated Parmesan cheese (optional)

Prepare linguini according to package directions, omitting salt and oil. Drain. Return to pan and toss with pesto sauce. Serve with Parmesan cheese.

Yield: 6 cups (6 servings)
One serving: 1 cup
Per serving: 253 calories, 42 grams carbohydrate, 8 grams protein, 6 grams fat
Exchanges: 2 ½ starch, 1 fat

Rice and Bean Burritos

Those who enjoy South-of-the-Border flavor will enjoy this tasty dish.

2 Tbl. salsa, thick and chunky
1/3 cup water
1 green bell pepper, finely diced
1 can (16 oz.) diced tomatoes, not drained*
3/4 cup quick-cooking brown rice, uncooked
1/4 tsp. dried thyme
1/4 tsp. salt (optional)
1/8 tsp. pepper
1 can (15 oz.) black beans, drained and rinsed
8 flour tortillas (7 1/2" diameter)
light sour cream (optional)
salsa, thick and chunky (optional)

Spray a large skillet with non-stick cooking spray. Add salsa, water, green bell pepper, tomatoes, rice, and seasonings. Bring to a boil. Reduce heat to low. Cover and simmer 15 minutes. Stir in drained beans. Continue to cook on low, covered, for 10 minutes or until most of the liquid is absorbed, stirring occasionally.

Warm tortillas in microwave oven on high, in a covered microwave-safe container, for 1 minute, rotating 1/4 turn halfway through cooking time. Or, heat in the oven, wrapped in aluminum foil, for 10 minutes at 350 degrees. Serve 1/2 cup filling in each tortilla. Top with optional light sour cream and/or salsa before folding.

Yield: about 4 cups filling and 8 tortillas (8 servings)
One serving: 1 tortilla and 1/2 cup filling
Per serving: 199 calories, 36 grams carbohydrate, 7 grams protein, 3 grams fat
Exchanges: 2 starch, 1 vegetable

*Sodium is figured for salt-free.

Vegetable Lasagna

You save time with this recipe because you don't precook the noodles. It is very attractive and a great way to use fresh garden vegetables.

Béchamel Sauce:
2 cups skim milk, divided
2 Tbl. unbleached flour
2 oz. grated part-skim mozzarella cheese
1/2 cup grated Parmesan cheese
1/8 tsp. dried oregano
1/8 tsp. nutmeg

4 cups spaghetti sauce (less than 4g fat per 4 oz.)
1 small eggplant (about 12 oz.), peeled and sliced thin
12 oz. lasagna noodles, dry
1 1/2 cups thinly sliced fresh vegetables such as broccoli, carrots and zucchini
1 package (10 oz.) frozen leaf spinach, thawed and drained

Prepare Béchamel sauce: Pour 1/2 cup of milk in a covered container. Add flour and shake well to prevent lumps. In a glass measuring cup, mix flour mixture with remaining milk and cook on high in the microwave for 5 minutes, or until thickened, stirring every 60 seconds to prevent lumping. Add the remaining sauce ingredients. Set aside.

Preheat oven to 350 degrees. In a 9" x 13" pan that has been sprayed with non-stick cooking spray, pour in 1/3 spaghetti sauce and layer in this order: eggplant, 1/3 lasagna noodles, 1/3 spaghetti sauce, fresh vegetables, 1/3 lasagna noodles, Béchamel sauce, spinach, the remainder of the lasagna noodles and the remainder of the spaghetti sauce. Cover tightly with aluminum foil and bake for one hour.

Yield: 8 servings
One serving: 1/8 of recipe
Per serving: 309 calories, 52 grams carbohydrate, 15 grams protein, 4 grams fat
Exchanges: 2 1/2 starch, 1/2 medium-fat meat, 3 vegetable

$\mathcal{P}$oultry

The variety of recipes in this section offers more ways to prepare lean poultry. Be sure to keep boneless, skinless chicken breasts in your freezer so you can prepare a meal on a very short notice. You'll find additional poultry recipes in the sections on *Sandwiches*, *Soups and Stews* and *Salads*.

Most of the recipes have a notation stating that the calories are less than the *Exchanges* would compute. This is because chicken breasts have about one gram of fat per ounce instead of the three grams of fat used in the *Exchange List* for the lean meat group.

Chicken and Black Bean Burritos

A quick meal that the whole family will enjoy. This goes especially well with Citrus Salad on page 100. Kidney beans or pinto beans can be substituted for the black beans. Leftover filling is also good served cold on lettuce.

½ lb. skinless, boneless chicken breasts, cut in bite-size pieces
1 tsp. cumin
1 tsp. garlic powder
1 can (15 oz.) black beans, drained and rinsed
1 can (8 oz.) whole kernel corn, drained*
½ cup salsa, thick and chunky
1 green bell pepper, diced
6 flour tortillas (7 ½" diameter)
light sour cream (optional)
salsa, thick and chunky (optional)

Brown chicken in a skillet that has been sprayed with non-stick cooking spray. Add all but the tortillas and continue to cook until the chicken is done. Heat tortillas in a covered microwave-safe container in the microwave for 1 minute rotating ¼ turn halfway through cooking.

To serve, spoon ¾ cup of chicken mixture onto a tortilla. Fold ends in and roll up burrito style. Serve as is or with salsa and light sour cream.

Yield: 6 servings
One serving: ¾ cup mixture and one tortilla
Per serving: 239 calories, 35 grams carbohydrate, 16 grams protein, 4 grams fat
Exchanges: 2 starch, 1 lean meat, 1 vegetable

*Sodium is figured for salt-free.

Chicken and Red Pepper Burritos

This is a simple dish that will be enjoyed by the entire family. Serve salsa and light sour cream as a topping.

½ lb. skinless, boneless chicken breasts, cut in bite-size pieces
½ red bell pepper, chopped
2 Tbl. chopped onion
1 tsp. chopped garlic
½ tsp. dried cilantro
½ tsp. dried basil
¼ tsp. cumin
½ tomato, diced
2 oz. grated reduced-fat cheddar cheese
5 flour tortillas (7 ½" diameter)

Preheat oven to 350 degrees. Spray skillet with non-stick cooking spray. Over medium heat, sauté chicken, bell pepper, onion, garlic and seasonings until chicken is cooked. Mix in tomatoes and cheese. Spoon filling onto each tortilla. Roll tightly, and place seam side down in 8" x 8" baking dish that has been sprayed with non-stick cooking spray. Bake 15 minutes or until heated through.

Yield: 5 servings
One serving: 1 filled tortilla
Per serving: 210 calories, 22 grams carbohydrate, 17 grams protein, 6 grams fat
Exchanges: 1 starch, 2 lean meat, 1 vegetable

Chicken á la King

Use leftover chicken or turkey in this simple dish. Serve over hot biscuits, toast, noodles or rice.

3 Tbl. unbleached flour
1 ¹/₂ cups skim milk, divided
1 ¹/₂ tsp. instant chicken bouillon*
2 cups cooked and cubed chicken or turkey
1 cup frozen peas
1 jar (2 oz.) pimento
¹/₈ tsp. pepper

Combine flour with ¹/₂ cup cold milk in covered container and shake well to prevent lumps. Follow directions below for stove top or microwave oven.

Stove Top: Pour into a saucepan along with the rest of the milk and the chicken bouillon. Bring to a boil, stirring constantly until thickened. Lower heat and add remaining ingredients. Continue cooking until peas and chicken are heated.

Microwave Oven: Pour into a 2-quart microwave-safe casserole along with the rest of the milk and the chicken bouillon. Cook on high for 5-6 minutes, stirring several times, until mixture thickens. Add remaining ingredients. Cover and continue to cook on high for 2-3 minutes or until peas and chicken are heated throughout.

Yield: 3 cups (4 servings)
One serving: ³/₄ cup
Per serving: 214 calories, 16 grams carbohydrate, 29 grams protein, 4 grams fat
Exchanges**: ¹/₂ milk, ¹/₂ starch, 3 ¹/₂ lean meat

*Sodium is figured for salt-free.

**Due to the low fat content of chicken breasts, calories are less than the exchanges would compute.

Chicken Chop Suey

This is an easy dish that tastes great over noodles or rice. You can substitute leftover turkey which makes this a good choice after Thanksgiving.

1 lb. skinless, boneless chicken breasts, cut in strips (or 2 cups cooked, cubed chicken or turkey)
2 cups sliced celery
1 cup sliced onion
1 cup chicken broth, fat removed*
1 Tbl. soy sauce
1/4 tsp. salt (optional)
2 1/2 Tbl. cornstarch
1/4 tsp. ginger
1 Tbl. molasses
1/4 cup water
1 can (16 oz.) bean sprouts, drained (or 1 1/2 cups fresh)

Spray a large frying pan with non-stick cooking spray and brown chicken (if using cooked meat, there is no need to brown). Add celery, onion, broth, soy sauce and salt (optional). Cover and simmer for 5-10 minutes. Meanwhile, mix cornstarch, ginger, molasses and water. Stir into hot mixture and cook until thickened. Add bean sprouts and heat thoroughly. Serve over noodles or quick-cooking brown rice.

Yield: 5 cups (4 servings)
One serving: 1 1/4 cup
Per serving: 197 calories, 15 grams carbohydrate, 28 grams protein, 3 grams fat
Exchanges**: 3 1/2 lean meat, 3 vegetable

*Sodium is figured for salt-free.

**Due to the low fat content of chicken breasts, calories are less than the exchanges would compute.

Chicken Curry

This spicy dish will appeal to anyone who likes curry. Use the lesser amount of curry if you do not like spicy-hot dishes.

¾ lb. skinless, boneless chicken breasts, cut in strips
1 medium onion, chopped
1 Tbl. chopped garlic
1-2 Tbl. curry
1 ½ cups diced apple
¼ tsp. salt (optional)
1 ½ cups chicken broth, fat removed, divided*
2 Tbl. unbleached flour
2 cups cooked brown rice (use quick-cooking)

Spray skillet with non-stick cooking spray. Stir-fry chicken with onion and garlic until chicken is browned. Add curry, apple, salt (optional) and 1 cup of broth. Cover and simmer for 10 minutes or until chicken is done. In a covered container, shake flour with ½ cup of broth to prevent lumps. Stir into chicken mixture and bring to a boil, stirring constantly until thickened. Serve over cooked rice.

Yield: 4 cups Chicken Curry and 2 cups rice (4 servings)
One serving: 1 cup Chicken Curry and ½ cup rice
Per serving: 278 calories, 37 grams carbohydrate, 24 grams protein, 3 grams fat
Exchanges**: 2 starch, 2 ½ lean meat, ½ fruit

*Sodium is figured for salt-free.

**Due to the low fat content of chicken breasts, calories are less than the exchanges would compute.

Chicken Fricassee

The sherry adds a special flavor to this popular dish. However, chicken broth can be substituted for the sherry. Serve over rice, mashed potatoes or noodles.

1 lb. skinless, boneless chicken breasts, cut in strips
1 cup sliced onions
1 cup sliced mushrooms
1 bell pepper, sliced (red or green)
1 ½ cups chicken broth, fat removed*
1 tsp. lemon juice
½ tsp. dried thyme
¼ tsp. salt (optional)
½ cup skim milk
4 Tbl. unbleached flour
3 Tbl. sherry

Spray skillet with non-stick cooking spray. Over medium heat, stir-fry chicken with onions, mushrooms and bell pepper until chicken is lightly browned. Add all but the last three ingredients. Cover and simmer for 10 minutes. Meanwhile, in a covered container, shake milk with flour to prevent lumps. Stir into chicken along with the sherry. Bring to a boil, stirring constantly until thickened.

Yield: 4 cups (4 servings)
One serving: 1 cup
Per serving: 216 calories, 14 grams carbohydrate, 30 grams protein, 3 grams fat
Exchanges**: ½ starch, 3 ½ lean meat, 1 vegetable

*Sodium is figured for salt-free.

**Due to the low fat content of chicken breasts, calories are less than the exchanges would compute.

Chicken Hungarian Goulash

This is an attractive and simple dish. Serve this with a tossed salad. Beef or pork can be substituted for the chicken.

4 ½ oz. ziti pasta - tube shape (about 1 ½ cups dry)
1 lb. skinless, boneless chicken breasts, cut in bite-size pieces
1 medium onion, chopped
1 medium green pepper, chopped
1 can (16 oz.) diced tomatoes, not drained*
1 can (8 oz.) tomato sauce*
1 Tbl. paprika
1 Tbl. dried parsley
½ tsp. salt (optional)
⅛ tsp. pepper

Cook noodles according to package directions, omitting salt and oil. Drain and set aside. Meanwhile, spray skillet with non-stick cooking spray. Add chicken, onion and green pepper and stir-fry until browned. Add remaining ingredients, including noodles, and heat thoroughly.

Yield: 6 cups (4 servings)
One serving: 1 ½ cups
Per serving: 315 calories, 38 grams carbohydrate, 32 grams protein, 4 grams fat
Exchanges**: 2 starch, 3 lean meat, 2 vegetable

Variation: Beef Hungarian Goulash - Substitute 1 lb. top sirloin for the chicken.

*Sodium is figured for salt-free.

**Due to the low fat content of chicken breasts, calories are less than the exchanges would compute.

Chicken Medley

This is a colorful dish that can be varied by using different vegetables and meats. It's great served over rice or noodles.

1 lb. skinless, boneless chicken breasts, cut in strips
1 package (6 oz.) frozen pea pods, thawed and drained
2 cups sliced celery
1 red bell pepper, sliced
½ cup sliced onion
2 cups chicken broth, fat removed*
1 tsp. soy sauce
¼ tsp. ground ginger
¼ tsp. salt (optional)
3 Tbl. cornstarch
½ cup water

Brown chicken in a skillet that has been sprayed with non-stick cooking spray. Add all but the last two ingredients and simmer, covered, until chicken is tender, about 10 minutes. Meanwhile, mix cornstarch with water. Stir into hot mixture and simmer, stirring constantly, until thickened. Serve over rice or noodles.

Yield: 6 cups (4 servings)
One serving: 1 ½ cups
Per serving: 220 calories, 17 grams carbohydrate, 31 grams protein, 3 grams fat
Exchanges**: ½ starch, 3 ½ lean meat, 2 vegetable

*Sodium is figured for salt-free.

**Due to the low fat content of chicken breasts, calories are less than the exchanges would compute.

Ramen Chicken

This is an entire meal in one pot. Substitute other vegetables for variety. It has an excellent taste and also looks appealing.

1 lb. skinless, boneless chicken breasts, cut in bite-size pieces
2 ³/₄ cups chicken broth, fat removed*
1 Tbl. soy sauce
1 tsp. ground ginger
¹/₈ tsp. pepper
¹/₄ tsp. salt (optional)
¹/₂ tsp. garlic powder
1 onion, cut in wedges
1 cup sliced mushrooms
¹/₂ cup sliced carrots
1 pkg. (6 oz.) frozen pea pods, thawed and drained
4 oz. coil vermicelli (fine noodles), dry
1 Tbl. cornstarch
¹/₄ cup water

Spray a skillet with non-stick cooking spray and stir-fry chicken until no longer pink. Add all but the last three ingredients to the skillet and bring to a boil. Add noodles. Reduce heat to low, cover, and simmer for 8 to 10 minutes or until vegetables are almost done. Mix cornstarch with water. Add to skillet. Bring to a boil, stirring until thickened.

Yield: 7 cups (4 servings)
One serving: 1 ³/₄ cups
Per serving: 318 calories, 36 grams carbohydrate, 35 grams protein, 4 grams fat
Exchanges**: 2 starch, 3 ¹/₂ lean meat, 1 vegetable

*Sodium is figured for salt-free.

**Due to the low fat content of chicken breasts, calories are less than the exchanges would compute.

Skillet Chicken with Tomatoes

This is a flavorful and easy top-of-the-stove dish. You can add a green vegetable to the pot to make a complete meal or serve with a tossed salad.

1 lb. skinless, boneless chicken breasts, cut in bite-size pieces
1 small onion, thinly sliced
1 carrot, sliced
1 celery stalk, sliced
2 tsp. chopped garlic
1 tsp. dried oregano
½ tsp. dried parsley
¼ tsp. salt (optional)
1 can (16 oz.) stewed tomatoes, not drained*
1 ½ cups chicken broth, fat removed*
2 cups sliced potatoes

Spray a skillet with non-stick cooking spray. Sauté chicken until browned. Add remaining ingredients to skillet and simmer over medium heat until potatoes are tender.

Yield: 6 cups (4 servings)
One serving: 1 ½ cups
Per serving: 306 calories, 37 grams carbohydrate, 31 grams protein, 3 grams fat
Exchanges**: 2 starch, 3 ½ lean meat, 2 vegetable

*Sodium is figured for salt-free.

**Due to the low fat content of chicken breasts, calories are less than the exchanges would compute.

Szechuan Chicken

Serve this great tasting Chinese dish with rice or low-fat Ramen noodles. If you like spicy-hot dishes, use the larger amount of Szechuan sauce.

1 lb. skinless, boneless chicken breasts, cut in bite-size pieces
¼ cup teriyaki sauce
2 tsp. chopped garlic
1 cup sliced red bell pepper
1 cup sliced green bell pepper
16 green onions, cut in 1-inch pieces
2-4 Tbl. Szechuan sauce
⅓ cup dry roasted peanuts, unsalted

Combine chicken with teriyaki sauce, and marinate at least 1 hour in the refrigerator. Drain and discard marinade. Spray a large skillet with non-stick cooking spray and stir-fry chicken with garlic until no longer pink. Add remaining ingredients except peanuts, and stir-fry for 1-2 minutes or until vegetables are tender. Add peanuts.

Yield: 6 cups (4 servings)
One serving: 1 ½ cups
Per serving: 232 calories, 9 grams carbohydrate, 30 grams protein, 9 grams fat
Exchanges: 3 ½ lean meat, 2 vegetable

Black Bean and Chicken Casserole

This dish has excellent flavor. Kidney beans can be substituted for black beans.

1 lb. skinless, boneless chicken breasts, cut in strips
$1/4$ tsp. each: salt (optional) and chili powder
$1/8$ tsp. pepper
1 cup quick-cooking brown rice, uncooked
1 $1/4$ cups chicken broth, fat removed*
1 can (15 oz.) black beans, drained and rinsed
1 can (4 oz.) diced green chiles
$1/8$ tsp. each: cumin, cayenne pepper, and garlic powder
$1/4$ tsp. each: onion powder and dried oregano
2 oz. reduced-fat cheddar cheese, grated

Spray a 9″ x 13″ baking pan, or microwave-safe dish, with non-stick cooking spray. Arrange chicken in pan and top with salt (optional), chili powder, and pepper. Follow directions below for conventional oven or microwave.

Conventional Oven: Preheat oven to 350 degrees. Bake for 20 minutes or until chicken is done.

Microwave Oven: Cover with plastic wrap. Cook on high for 6-8 minutes, depending on thickness of chicken. Rotate dish halfway through cooking time.

Meanwhile, cook rice according to package directions, substituting chicken broth for water and omitting salt and butter. When rice is done, mix in black beans, chiles and remaining seasonings. Pour drippings from cooked chicken into rice mixture and mix well. Spread over chicken. Top with grated cheese. Return to conventional oven for 5 minutes (microwave oven for 30 seconds) or until cheese is melted.

Yield: about 6 cups (5 servings)
One serving: 1 $1/4$ cups
Per serving: 272 calories, 26 grams carbohydrate, 31 grams protein, 5 grams fat
Exchanges**: 2 starch, 3 $1/2$ lean meat

*Sodium is figured for salt-free.

**Due to the low fat content of chicken breasts, calories are less than the exchanges would compute.

Chicken and Broccoli in Cheese Sauce

The addition of rice and vegetables makes this one dish meal great tasting and colorful. Asparagus or brussel sprouts can be used in place of the broccoli spears for variety.

1 cup quick-cooking brown rice, uncooked
1/2 cup finely chopped onion
1/2 cup finely chopped celery
1 Tbl. dried parsley
1 tsp. instant chicken bouillon*
1/4 tsp. dried thyme
1 cup of boiling water
1 lb. skinless, boneless chicken breasts, cut in strips
4 cups broccoli spears

<u>Cheese Sauce</u>
1 1/2 cups cold skim milk, divided
3 Tbl. unbleached flour
1/4 tsp. salt (optional)
1/8 tsp. pepper
3 oz. reduced-fat sharp cheddar cheese, cut in small pieces

Preheat oven to 450 degrees. Spray a 9" x 13" baking pan with non-stick cooking spray. Add rice, onion, celery, parsley, bouillon, thyme and water, stirring to mix well. Top with chicken breasts and broccoli spears. Cover with aluminum foil and bake for 30 minutes, or until chicken is no longer pink.

Meanwhile, prepare cheese sauce. Combine 1/2 cup milk with flour in covered container and shake well to prevent lumps. Pour into a 4-cup glass measuring cup along with the rest of the milk and seasonings. Cook in the microwave on high for 4 to 5 minutes, stirring with a wire whisk every 60 seconds until mixture thickens. Mix in the cheese and stir until melted. Pour sauce over broccoli and chicken before serving.

Yield: 5 servings
One serving: $^1/_5$ recipe
Per serving: 302 calories, 27 grams carbohydrate, 34 grams protein, 6 grams fat
Exchanges**: 1 $^1/_2$ starch, 4 lean meat, 1 vegetable

*Sodium is figured for salt-free.

**Due to the low fat content of chicken breasts, calories are less than the exchanges would compute.

Chicken and Stuffing Casserole

A special meal and definitely a family favorite. You can easily substitute leftover turkey for the chicken.

1 cup chopped onion
1 cup chopped celery
1 ½ cups chicken broth, fat removed*
6 cups (6 oz.) packaged unseasoned stuffing mix (cubes)
½ tsp. dried thyme
½ tsp. dried sage
⅛ tsp. dried marjoram
1 lb. skinless, boneless chicken breasts, cut in strips
1 cup chicken broth, fat removed*
2 Tbl. unbleached flour
1 Tbl. dried parsley

Preheat oven to 350 degrees. In a medium saucepan, combine onion, celery and broth. Simmer, covered, on low until vegetables are soft. Add stuffing and seasonings. Mix well until blended. Spread in an 8" x 8" pan that has been sprayed with non-stick cooking spray. Top with chicken strips.

Meanwhile, in a covered container, combine chicken broth with flour and shake well to prevent lumps. Pour into a 4-cup glass measuring cup and cook in the microwave on high for 3 minutes, stirring with a wire whisk several times until mixture thickens. Pour over chicken breasts. Sprinkle with parsley. Cover and bake for 30 minutes or until chicken is no longer pink.

Yield: 4 servings
One serving: ¼ recipe
Per serving: 345 calories, 40 grams carbohydrate, 35 grams protein, 5 grams fat
Exchanges**: 2 starch, 3 ½ lean meat, 1 vegetable

Variation: Use leftover cooked turkey and reduce the cooking time to 20 minutes or until all ingredients are thoroughly heated.

*Sodium is figured for salt-free.

**Due to the low fat content of chicken breasts, calories are less than the exchanges would compute.

Chicken Noodle Casserole

This is a simple pasta dish which uses fresh chicken or you can easily substitute leftover turkey or chicken. Serve with a green vegetable.

8 oz. rotini noodles - corkscrew shape (about 3 cups dry)
1 lb. skinless, boneless chicken breasts, cut in bite-size pieces
¹/₂ cup chopped celery
¹/₂ cup chopped onion
1 cup chicken broth, fat removed*
1 jar (2 oz.) pimento
2 Tbl. dried parsley
¹/₂ tsp. garlic powder
¹/₂ tsp. dried thyme
¹/₂ tsp. salt (optional)
¹/₈ tsp. pepper

Prepare noodles according to package directions, omitting salt and oil. Drain and set aside. In a skillet that has been sprayed with non-stick cooking spray, brown chicken, celery and onion. Add the remaining ingredients and simmer on low until meat is tender and vegetables are cooked. Mix in noodles and continue to simmer on low until half of the liquid is absorbed. Remove from heat, cover, and let sit for 5 minutes before serving.

Yield: 8 cups (5 servings)
One serving: about 1 ¹/₂ cups
Per serving: 285 calories, 37 grams carbohydrate, 27 grams protein, 3 grams fat
Exchanges**: 2 ¹/₂ starch, 2 ¹/₂ lean meat

Variation: Add 1 cup of sliced mushrooms and sauté with the celery and onion.

*Sodium is figured for salt-free.

**Due to the low fat content of chicken breasts, calories are less than the exchanges would compute.

Patio Chicken and Rice

This meal-in-a-pot is great for company. It takes only minutes to assemble and requires no attention while baking. You can eliminate the carrots and serve with a tossed salad or you can change the vegetable to another such as broccoli and add during the last half hour of cooking.

2 Tbl. cornstarch
$1/4$ cup water
$1/2$ cup skim milk
1 cup chicken broth, fat removed*
$1/2$ tsp. pepper
$1/4$ tsp. salt (optional)
$1/3$ cup dried chopped onion
1 $1/2$ cups quick-cooking brown rice, uncooked
1 cup chicken broth, fat removed*
1 can (8 oz.) sliced mushrooms, drained and rinsed
1 jar (2 oz.) pimento
8-10 skinless chicken parts (thighs, legs and breast quarters)
10 small (4") carrots, scrubbed
$1/2$ tsp. paprika

Preheat oven to 350 degrees. In a 4-cup glass measuring cup, mix cornstarch with water. Add milk and 1 cup of chicken broth. Heat on high in microwave for 7-9 minutes, stirring every 3 minutes until bubbly and thickened. Add the pepper, salt and onion. Set aside. Spread rice in a 4-quart Dutch oven that has been sprayed with non-stick cooking spray. Pour 1 cup of broth over rice. Top with mushrooms, pimento, chicken and carrots. Pour cornstarch mixture over all.

Sprinkle with paprika. Cover and bake 1 $1/4$ hours or until chicken is tender. Remove cover and bake another 10 minutes to brown.

Yield: 5 servings
One serving: 2 pieces of chicken and 1 cup of rice/carrots
Per serving: 373 calories, 42 grams carbohydrate, 34 grams protein, 7 grams fat
Exchanges: 2 starch, 3 $1/2$ lean meat, 2 vegetable

*Sodium is figured for salt-free.

Roast Chicken and Vegetables

Using a Dutch oven, or any type of covered baking pan, actually steams the chicken and the result is very tender meat cooked in a short period of time. The addition of vegetables completes this meal. Consider substituting zucchini and green bell pepper as these taste great cooked with chicken. The drippings can be thickened to make a delicious gravy.

4-5 lb. whole fryer chicken
1 stalk celery, cut in sticks
½ onion, quartered
4 small potatoes, cut in half
2 medium carrots, cut in 3" pieces

<u>Optional gravy</u>
drippings, fat removed
unbleached flour

Preheat oven to 400 degrees. Prepare chicken by removing giblets and neck. Rinse entire bird, including cavity. Remove any visible fat. Stuff cavity with celery and onion. Set on a rack in a covered baking pan that has been sprayed with non-stick cooking spray. If using a meat thermometer, insert in breast, without it touching the bone. Cover and bake for 30 minutes.

Add potatoes and carrots, being careful not to have them sit in the juices. Cover and cook for 30 to 45 minutes until chicken is cooked. Chicken is done if the drumstick moves easily. If using a meat thermometer, it should register 190 degrees. Remove skin when carving.

Drain and reserve the liquid. Discard the fat which will rise to the top. Thicken the liquid for a gravy by adding flour. Add 2 Tbl. of flour, mixed in ¼ cup of cold water, to each cup of liquid. Cook on the stove top or in the microwave, stirring frequently, until bubbly and thickened.

Yield: 4 servings
One serving: ¼ recipe
Per serving: 405 calories, 39 grams carbohydrate, 37 grams protein, 11 grams fat
Exchanges: 2 starch, 3 ½ lean meat, 2 vegetable

Teriyaki Chicken Breasts

The marinade gives a wonderful flavor to this dish. Jumbo shrimp can be substituted for the chicken.

⅓ cup soy sauce
½ cup water
2 Tbl. brown sugar (or the equivalent in artificial sweetener)
1 tsp. ground ginger
½ tsp. garlic powder
1 lb. skinless, boneless chicken breasts

Mix the soy sauce, water, sugar, ginger and garlic powder in a shallow bowl. Add chicken and marinate for 1 to 2 hours in the refrigerator. Drain chicken and discard marinade.

Barbecue: Start barbecue. When hot, place chicken on grill. Close hood and cook for 8-10 minutes, turning the chicken halfway through the cooking time. Be sure to cook until chicken is no longer pink.

Conventional Oven: Preheat oven to 350 degrees. Bake, uncovered, for 25-30 minutes until chicken is no longer pink.

Broiler: Preheat broiler. Place chicken on the broiler pan about 3-4 inches from the heat. Broil for 4 minutes. Turn chicken and broil for an additional 4 minutes or until chicken is no longer pink.

Yield: 4 servings
One serving: ¼ recipe
Per serving: 132 calories, 1 gram carbohydrate, 25 grams protein, 3 grams fat
Exchanges*: 3 ½ lean meat

*Due to the low fat content of chicken breasts, calories are less than the exchanges would compute.

Chicken Cordon Bleu

You'll find this dish attractive, easy to prepare, and a good choice for company. I use packaged cornflake crumbs in this recipe.

4 skinless, boneless chicken breasts (about 1 lb.)
4 thin slices of low-fat ham (about ¹/₂ oz. each)
2 Tbl. skim milk
¹/₄ cup cornflake crumbs
2 oz. reduced-fat Swiss cheese

Preheat oven to 400 degrees. Cut a pocket in each breast and tuck in one slice of ham. Roll in milk and then cornflake crumbs. Arrange in an 8" x 8" pan that has been sprayed with non-stick cooking spray. Bake for 25 minutes. Top each breast with ¹/₂ oz. of cheese and return to oven until cheese is melted.

Yield: 4 servings
One serving: ¹/₄ recipe
Per serving: 218 calories, 7 grams carbohydrate, 33 grams protein, 6 grams fat
Exchanges*: ¹/₂ starch, 4 ¹/₂ lean meat

*Due to the low fat content of chicken breasts, calories are less than the exchanges would compute.

Chicken Parmesan

This recipe makes a delicious sauce that tastes great over noodles.

1 cup spaghetti sauce (less than 4g fat per 4 oz.), divided
1 lb. skinless, boneless chicken breasts
½ green bell pepper, sliced
½ cup sliced onion
8 oz. fettucini noodles, dry
2 oz. grated part-skim mozzarella cheese
grated Parmesan cheese (optional)

Spray an 8″x8″ pan, or microwave-safe dish, with non-stick cooking spray. Pour ½ cup of sauce in the pan. Place chicken in pan and top with vegetables and remaining sauce. Follow directions below for microwave or conventional oven.

Conventional Oven: Preheat oven to 350 degrees. Cover with aluminum foil and bake for 30-40 minutes.

Microwave Oven: Cover with plastic wrap. Cook on high for 10 minutes, depending on thickness of chicken. Rotate ¼ turn halfway through cooking.

Meanwhile, prepare noodles according to package directions, omitting oil and salt. Top chicken with mozzarella cheese and return to oven, uncovered, until cheese is melted (conventional oven about 5 minutes or microwave about 40 seconds). Serve with noodles. Pass the Parmesan cheese (optional).

Yield: 4 servings
One serving: ¼ recipe
Per serving: 407 calories, 50 grams carbohydrate, 37 grams protein, 6 grams fat
Exchanges*: 3 starch, 3 ½ lean meat, 1 vegetable

*Due to the low fat content of chicken breasts, calories are less than the exchanges would compute.

Creamy Chicken Dijon

The rich tasting sauce makes this an extra special chicken recipe. It's a family favorite in my home and it is definitely a good choice for company.

3 Tbl. light mayonnaise
2 Tbl. nonfat plain yogurt
2 tsp. Dijon mustard
1 tsp. honey
1 lb. skinless, boneless chicken breasts
1 tsp. dried parsley

Mix mayonnaise, yogurt, mustard and honey to make the sauce. Set aside. Follow the directions for microwave or conventional oven.

Microwave Oven: Arrange chicken in an 8" x 8" microwave-safe dish that has been sprayed with non-stick cooking spray. Cover with plastic wrap. Cook on high for 6-8 minutes, rotating $1/4$ turn halfway through cooking time. The time will vary depending on the thickness of the chicken. Drain the liquid, reserving 3 tablespoons. Mix the 3 tablespoons of reserved liquid with the sauce and pour over the chicken. Sprinkle with parsley. Cover and cook for 1-2 minutes or until chicken is no longer pink and the sauce is heated.

Conventional Oven: Preheat oven to 350 degrees. Arrange chicken in an 8" x 8" pan that has been sprayed with non-stick cooking spray. Bake chicken, covered, for 20 minutes. Drain the liquid, reserving 3 tablespoons. Mix the 3 tablespoons of reserved liquid with the sauce and pour over the chicken. Sprinkle with parsley. Return to oven for 5 minutes or until chicken is no longer pink and the sauce is heated.

Yield: 4 servings
One serving: $1/4$ recipe
Per serving: 174 calories, 3 grams carbohydrate, 26 grams protein, 6 grams fat
Exchanges*: 3 $1/2$ lean meat

*Due to the low fat content of chicken breasts, calories are less than the exchanges would compute.

Spanish Chicken

This colorful dish is especially good served with our Spanish Rice and Beans recipe on page 126. Think about following the barbecue method on a hot summer night.

1 lb. skinless, boneless chicken breasts
3 green onions, chopped
1 tomato, chopped
1 can (4 oz.) diced green chiles
¼ tsp. salt (optional)
⅛ tsp. cumin
⅛ tsp. pepper

Conventional Oven: Preheat oven to 350 degrees. Spray an 8" x 8" pan with non-stick cooking spray. Arrange chicken in the pan. Top with remaining ingredients. Bake uncovered for 25-35 minutes or until chicken is done.

Barbecue or Broiling: Barbecue or broil chicken about 3-4 minutes on each side or until done. Mix remaining ingredients and cook on high in microwave until heated throughout, about 2 minutes. Pour over cooked chicken.

Microwave Oven: Arrange chicken in an 8" x 8" microwave-safe dish that has been sprayed with non-stick cooking spray. Top with remaining ingredients. Cover with plastic wrap. Cook on high for 6-8 minutes, rotating ¼ turn halfway through cooking time. Time will vary with thickness of chicken.

Yield: 4 servings
One serving: ¼ recipe
Per serving: 147 calories, 4 grams carbohydrate, 26 grams protein, 3 grams fat
Exchanges*: 3 ½ lean meat, 1 vegetable

*Due to the low fat content of chicken breasts, calories are less than the exchanges would compute.

Aloha Chicken

You'll find this to be another good recipe for chicken breasts. The pineapple adds a sweetness to this dish.

1 small can (8 oz.) unsweetened pineapple slices, packed in juice
1 tsp. chopped garlic
1 tsp. cornstarch
1 tsp. Worcestershire sauce
1 tsp. Dijon mustard
½ tsp. dried thyme
4 skinless, boneless chicken breasts (about 1 lb.)

Preheat oven to 400 degrees. Drain pineapple, reserving the juice. Combine juice with garlic, cornstarch, Worcestershire, mustard and thyme. Arrange chicken in an 8" x 8" pan that has been sprayed with non-stick cooking spray. Pour juice mixture over chicken and bake for 20 minutes. Spoon juices from pan over chicken. Add a pineapple slice to each chicken piece and return to the oven for 5 minutes.

Yield: 4 servings
One serving: ¼ recipe
Per serving: 172 calories, 10 grams carbohydrate, 26 grams protein, 3 grams fat
Exchanges*: 3 ½ lean meat, ½ fruit

*Due to the low fat content of chicken breasts, calories are less than the exchanges would compute.

Chili Tamale Pie

If you like cornmeal, you'll like this dish. Homemade chili can be substituted for canned, and it will significantly reduce the sodium. Serve this with coleslaw or a fruit salad.

2 ½ cups water
1 tsp. salt (optional)
1 ¼ cups yellow cornmeal
2 cans (15 oz. each) reduced-fat turkey chili with beans*
2 oz. grated reduced-fat cheddar cheese

Preheat oven to 350 degrees. Combine water, salt (optional) and cornmeal in a saucepan. Cook over medium heat, stirring frequently, for about 10 minutes until thick and stiff. Pour into an 8" x 8" baking pan that has been sprayed with non-stick cooking spray. Top with chili and bake for 25 minutes. Sprinkle with cheese and return to oven for 5 minutes or until cheese is melted.

Yield: 6 servings
One serving: ¹/₆ recipe
Per serving: 254 calories, 39 grams carbohydrate, 15 grams protein, 4 grams fat
Exchanges: 2 ½ starch, 1 lean meat

*or choose another canned chili with less than 30% fat (about 8 grams of fat per 220 Calories)

Seafood

This section presents a number of recipes that give you the choice of using fish fillets, shrimp and/or scallops. Use different seafoods to provide variety in your diet. The general recommendation is to eat seafood three times a week. You'll find additional seafood recipes in the sections on *Sandwiches*, *Soups and Stews* and *Salads*.

Most of the recipes have a notation stating that the calories are less than the *Exchanges* would compute. This is because white fish has about one half gram of fat per ounce instead of the three grams of fat used in the *Exchange List* for the lean meat group.

Barbecued Fish Oriental

This recipe won a Blue Ribbon at the Wasco County Fair. It was prepared by 10-year-old Chris, the son of our recipe tester, Mary Beth Thouvenel. This marinade works well with salmon, halibut and sole.

1 lb. fish fillets
1/4 cup orange juice
1 Tbl. soy sauce
2 Tbl. water
2 Tbl. ketchup
1 Tbl. honey
1 Tbl. dried parsley
1/2 tsp. ginger
1/4 tsp. pepper

Cut fish into fillets and place in a single layer in a shallow pan. Combine the remaining ingredients, mix well and pour over the fish. Marinate for 30 minutes to one hour in the refrigerator, turning the fillets once or twice to be sure they are well coated. Drain marinade.

Broil: Preheat oven to broil. Spray broiler pan with non-stick cooking spray. Arrange fish on pan. Broil 2"-3" from heat until done.

Barbecue: *Before starting the barbecue, spray aluminum foil with non-stick cooking spray. Place over rack, poking holes in several areas. Start barbecue. When ready, place fish on foil, close lid, and barbecue until done. Allow 10 minutes per inch of thickness.

Yield: 4 servings
One serving: 1/4 recipe
Per serving: 137 calories, 7 grams carbohydrate, 23 grams protein, 1 gram fat
Exchanges**: 3 1/2 lean meat, 1/2 fruit

*Note: Non-stick cooking spray is flammable. Do not spray near open flame or heated surfaces.

**Due to the low fat content of fish, calories are less than the exchanges would compute.

Curried Sole

Curry adds an Eastern touch to traditional baked fish. This is a good dish to serve to company.

1 lb. fillets of sole
¼ cup light mayonnaise
1 tsp. lemon juice
1 tsp. curry
1 Tbl. dried parsley

Arrange fish in a 9″ x 13″ baking pan, or microwave-safe dish, that has been sprayed with non-stick cooking spray. Set aside. Meanwhile, mix mayonnaise, lemon juice and curry. Spread on fillets. Sprinkle with parsley. Follow directions below for microwave or conventional oven.

Conventional Oven: Preheat oven to 450 degrees. Bake for 4-5 minutes per half-inch thickness of fish or until fish flakes easily with a fork.

Microwave Oven: Cover with plastic wrap. Cook on high for 4-6 minutes, depending on thickness of fish. Rotate dish halfway through cooking.

Yield: 4 servings
One serving: ¼ recipe
Per serving: 147 calories, 2 grams carbohydrate, 21 grams protein, 6 grams fat
Exchanges: 3 lean meat

Dijon Fillets

If you like the flavor of Dijon mustard, you'll like this simple fish recipe.

1 lb. fish fillets (such as sole or cod)
2 Tbl. light mayonnaise
1 Tbl. Dijon mustard
1 tsp. lemon juice
½ tsp. paprika

Arrange fish in a 9" x 13" baking pan, or microwave-safe dish, that has been sprayed with non-stick cooking spray. Mix mayonnaise, mustard and lemon juice. Spread on fillets. Sprinkle with paprika. Follow directions below for microwave or conventional oven.

Conventional Oven: Preheat oven to 450 degrees. Bake for 4-5 minutes per half-inch thickness of fish.

Microwave Oven: Cover with plastic wrap. Cook on high for 4-6 minutes, depending on thickness of fish. Rotate dish halfway through cooking.

Yield: 4 servings
One serving: ¼ recipe
Per serving: 135 calories, 1 gram carbohydrate, 23 grams protein, 4 grams fat
Exchanges*: 3 ½ lean meat

*Due to the low fat content of fish, calories are less than the exchanges would compute.

Fish Poached in Milk

This quick method for cooking fish also has a good flavor.

1 lb. fish fillets (halibut, snapper, sole)
¹/₂ cup skim milk
¹/₄ tsp. salt (optional)
¹/₈ tsp. pepper

Follow directions below for stove top or microwave method.

Stove Top: Arrange fish in a large skillet that has been sprayed with non-stick cooking spray. Pour milk over fish and sprinkle with seasonings. Cover and simmer for 1-4 minutes, depending on thickness, or until fish flakes easily with a fork. Remove fish with slotted spatula.

Microwave Oven: Arrange fish in a 9" x 13" microwave-safe dish that has been sprayed with non-stick cooking spray. Pour milk over fish and sprinkle with seasonings. Cover with plastic wrap. Cook on high for 4-6 minutes, depending on thickness of fish. Rotate dish halfway through cooking. Remove fish with slotted spatula.

Yield: 4 servings
One serving: ¹/₄ recipe
Per serving: 118 calories, 1 gram carbohydrate, 24 grams protein, 2 grams fat
Exchanges*: 3 ¹/₂ lean meat

*Due to the low fat content of fish, calories are less than the exchanges would compute.

Italian Baked Fish

You'll find this to be another easy way to prepare fish. Look for the cornflake crumbs in the grocery store on the same shelf as the bread crumbs and other breading products.

1 lb. fish fillets (sole, snapper, cod)
¼ cup nonfat Italian salad dressing
¼ cup cornflake crumbs

Preheat oven to 450 degrees. Marinate fish in dressing for 15 minutes in the refrigerator. Drain, reserving the marinade. Roll fish in cornflake crumbs. Arrange in a baking pan that has been sprayed with non-stick cooking spray. Drizzle remainder of marinade over fish. Bake for 4-5 minutes per half-inch thickness of fish or until fish flakes easily with a fork.

Yield: 4 servings
One serving: ¼ recipe
Per serving: 142 calories, 8 grams carbohydrate, 24 grams protein, 1 gram fat
Exchanges*: ½ starch, 3 ½ lean meat

*Due to the low fat content of fish, calories are less than the exchanges would compute.

Mushroom-Topped Fillets

A tasty and easy way to prepare fish.

1 lb. fish fillets (such as sole or cod)
1 Tbl. lemon juice
¹/₂ cup chopped onion
1 cup sliced mushrooms
1 Tbl. dried parsley
¹/₄ tsp. salt (optional)
¹/₈ tsp. pepper

Spray a 9" x 13" pan, or microwave-safe dish, with non-stick cooking spray. Arrange fish in the pan and top with lemon juice. Meanwhile, in a skillet that has been sprayed with non-stick cooking spray, sauté the onions and mushrooms until barely done. Add parsley. Spoon over fish. Season with salt (optional) and pepper. Follow directions below for microwave or conventional oven.

Conventional Oven: Preheat oven to 400 degrees. Bake for 10-15 minutes or until fish flakes easily with a fork.

Microwave Oven: Cover with plastic wrap. Cook on high for 6-8 minutes, depending on thickness of fish. Rotate dish halfway through cooking.

Yield: 4 servings
One serving: ¹/₄ recipe
Per serving: 122 calories, 3 grams carbohydrate, 24 grams protein, 2 grams fat
Exchanges*: 3 ¹/₂ lean meat

*Due to the low fat content of fish, calories are less than the exchanges would compute.

Parmesan Fish Fillets

This simple recipe has a flavorful breading that adds variety to baked fish.

¼ cup fine bread crumbs
¼ cup grated Parmesan cheese
½ tsp. dried thyme
¼ tsp. dried basil
⅛ tsp. onion powder
⅛ tsp. pepper
1 lb. white fish fillets (such as sole, cod, snapper)
¼ cup egg substitute (equal to 1 egg)
4 lemon wedges

Preheat oven to 400 degrees. Combine bread crumbs with Parmesan cheese and seasonings. Mix well. Dip fish in egg, and then coat with bread crumb mixture. Arrange on a baking sheet that has been sprayed with non-stick cooking spray. Bake for 10 minutes per inch of thickness, or until fish flakes easily with a fork. Serve with lemon wedges.

Yield: 4 servings
One serving: ¼ recipe
Per serving: 182 calories, 8 grams carbohydrate, 28 grams protein, 4 grams fat
Exchanges*: ½ starch, 4 lean meat

*Due to the low fat content of fish, calories are less than the exchanges would compute.

Stuffed Fish Fillets

This is a unique way to serve fish that is attractive. The Cheese Sauce on page 48 can be served with this dish.

$^{1}/_{2}$ cup chopped onion
$^{1}/_{2}$ cup chopped celery
$^{3}/_{4}$ cup chicken broth, fat removed*
3 cups (3 oz.) packaged unseasoned stuffing mix (cube type)
$^{1}/_{4}$ tsp. dried sage
$^{1}/_{4}$ tsp. dried thyme
1 lb. fish fillets, such as fillet of sole
$^{1}/_{4}$ tsp. paprika

Preheat oven to 350 degrees. In a medium saucepan, combine onion, celery and broth. Simmer, covered, on low until vegetables are soft. Add stuffing and seasonings. Mix well until blended. Place a heaping tablespoon of stuffing on each fish fillet. Roll the fillet around the stuffing and place seam side down in an 8" x 8" pan that has been sprayed with non-stick cooking spray. Sprinkle with paprika. Bake for 20 minutes or until fish flakes easily with a fork.

Yield: 4 servings
One serving: $^{1}/_{4}$ recipe
Per serving: 197 calories, 19 grams carbohydrate, 25 grams protein, 2 grams fat
Exchanges**: 1 starch, 3 lean meat

Variation: Serve with Cheese Sauce on page 48. After cooking the sauce, add $^{1}/_{4}$ to $^{1}/_{2}$ cup of small cooked shrimp.

*Sodium is figured for salt-free.

**Due to the low fat content of fish, calories are less than the exchanges would compute.

Zucchini Fish Bake

This is a colorful dish and a good one to prepare with a firm fish such as cod.

1 lb. firm fish fillets
2 small zucchini, thinly sliced
1 cup spaghetti sauce (less than 4g fat per 4 oz.)
1 Tbl. grated Parmesan cheese

Spray a 9" x 13" baking pan, or microwave-safe dish, with non-stick cooking spray. Arrange fillets in pan. Top with sliced zucchini. Spoon spaghetti sauce over fish. Sprinkle with Parmesan cheese. Follow directions below for conventional or microwave oven.

Conventional Oven: Preheat oven to 350 degrees. Cover and bake for 30 minutes or until fish is opaque and flakes easily with a fork. Serve with a slotted spoon.

Microwave Oven: Cover with plastic wrap. Cook on high for 8-12 minutes, depending on thickness of fish. Rotate dish halfway through cooking. Serve with a slotted spoon.

Yield: 4 servings
One serving: ¼ recipe
Per serving: 157 calories, 8 grams carbohydrate, 26 grams protein, 2 grams fat
Exchanges*: 3 ½ lean meat, 2 vegetable

*Due to the low fat content of fish, calories are less than the exchanges would compute.

Baked Fish and Rice with Dill Cheese Sauce

Another easy fish recipe. We especially like the flavor of the dill sauce.

1 cup quick-cooking brown rice, uncooked
1 cup boiling water
1 Tbl. dried parsley
1 tsp. instant chicken bouillon*
½ tsp. Italian seasoning
1 lb. fish fillets (such as cod or sole)
¼ tsp. paprika

<u>Dill Cheese Sauce</u>
3 Tbl. unbleached flour
1 ½ cups of skim milk, divided
2 tsp. dried dill weed
⅛ tsp. each: pepper and salt (optional)
3 oz. reduced-fat sharp cheddar cheese, cut in small pieces

Preheat oven to 375 degrees. Spray a 9" x 13" baking pan with non-stick cooking spray. Add rice, water, parsley, bouillon and Italian seasoning. Stir to mix. Cover with aluminum foil and bake for 10 minutes. Top rice with fish fillets. Sprinkle with paprika. Cover and return to oven for 15-20 minutes, until fish is opaque and flakes easily with a fork.

Meanwhile, prepare the sauce by combining the flour with ½ cup of milk in a covered container and shake well to prevent lumps. Pour into a 4-cup glass measuring cup along with the remainder of the milk and seasonings. Cook in the microwave on high for 4-5 minutes, or until thickened, stirring with a wire whisk every 60 seconds to prevent lumping. Add cheese and stir until melted. Pour over fish before serving.

Yield: 4 servings
One serving: ¼ recipe
Per serving: 314 calories, 27 grams carbohydrate, 37 grams protein, 6 grams fat
Exchanges**: ½ milk, 1 ½ starch, 4 lean meat

*Sodium is figured for salt-free.
**Due to the low fat content of fish, calories are less than the exchanges would compute.

Creamy Curried Seafood

This is another dish for people who really like curry. Vary or combine seafoods to suit your liking. Serve with rice.

½ cup thinly sliced onion
½ cup skim milk
2 Tbl. unbleached flour
1 tsp. curry
½ cup chicken broth, fat removed*
1 Tbl. dried parsley
¼ tsp. salt (optional)
1 lb. seafood, such as a firm fish (cod, halibut) cut in bite-size pieces, scallops, and/or shelled and deveined shrimp

Spray a skillet with non-stick cooking spray. Sauté onions until soft. Meanwhile, combine ½ cup milk with flour in covered container and shake well to prevent lumps. In the skillet add curry, flour mixture, broth and seasonings. Bring to a slow boil, stirring constantly until thickened. Reduce heat, add seafood, and simmer just until seafood is cooked. Serve over rice.

Yield: 2 cups (4 servings)
One serving: ½ cup
Per serving: 145 calories, 7 grams carbohydrate, 26 grams protein, 2 grams fat
Exchanges**: ½ starch, 3 ½ lean meat

*Sodium is figured for salt-free.

**Due to the low fat content of fish, calories are less than the exchanges would compute.

Creamy Seafood Fettucini

This is a special dish that you will enjoy serving to company or on special occasions. Jumbo shrimp is very good in this recipe as well as any combination of seafoods. Serve with fresh asparagus.

4 oz. egg noodles - "no yolk" type (about 3 cups dry)
1 ½ cups skim milk, divided
1 Tbl. dried parsley
½ tsp. garlic powder
¼ tsp. salt (optional)
¼ tsp. nutmeg
⅛ tsp. pepper
dash cayenne pepper
¼ cup grated Parmesan cheese
3 Tbl. dry sherry or white wine
3 Tbl. unbleached flour
1 lb. seafood, such as a firm fish (cod, halibut) cut in bite-size pieces, scallops, and/or shelled and deveined shrimp

Cook fettucini according to package directions, omitting salt and oil. Drain and keep warm. Meanwhile, spray a skillet with non-stick cooking spray. Pour 1 cup of milk in the skillet and add seasonings, Parmesan cheese and sherry or wine. Set over low heat. Meanwhile, in a covered container, shake flour with remaining ½ cup of milk to prevent lumps and add to the skillet. Bring to a slow boil, stirring constantly until thickened. Reduce heat, add seafood and simmer just until seafood is cooked. Toss with hot fettucini noodles.

Yield: 4 cups (4 servings)
One serving: 1 cup
Per serving: 310 calories, 32 grams carbohydrate, 33 grams protein, 4 grams fat
Exchanges*: ½ milk, 1 ½ starch, 3 ½ lean meat

*Due to the low fat content of fish, calories are less than the exchanges would compute.

Seafood Medley

This is a colorful dish that can be varied by using different vegetables. It's great served over rice or noodles.

1 package (6 oz.) frozen pea pods, thawed and drained
2 cups sliced celery
1 red bell pepper, sliced
$1/2$ cup sliced onion
1 tsp. soy sauce
$1/4$ tsp. ground ginger
$1/4$ tsp. salt (optional)
2 cups chicken broth, fat removed, divided*
3 Tbl. cornstarch
1 lb. seafood, such as a firm fish (cod, halibut) cut in bite-size pieces, scallops, and/or shelled and deveined shrimp

Spray a skillet with non-stick cooking spray. Add all ingredients except $1/2$ cup of the chicken broth, cornstarch and seafood. Simmer, covered, for 5 minutes. Meanwhile, mix cornstarch with remaining $1/2$ cup of broth. Stir into hot mixture and heat to a slow boil, stirring constantly, until thickened. Reduce heat, add seafood, and simmer until seafood is cooked. Do not overcook. Serve over rice or noodles.

Yield: 6 cups (4 servings)
One serving: 1 $1/2$ cups
Per serving: 186 calories, 14 grams carbohydrate, 28 grams protein, 2 grams fat
Exchanges**: $1/2$ starch, 3 $1/2$ lean meat, 1 vegetable

*Sodium is figured for salt-free.

**Due to the low fat content of fish, calories are less than the exchanges would compute.

Seafood Pasta

I like this recipe using Ziti noodles but any other noodle would also work. Serve with a tossed salad and Italian bread.

8 oz. ziti pasta - tube shape (about 3 cups dry)
1 Tbl. cornstarch
2 cans (16 oz. each) diced tomatoes, not drained*
1 Tbl. chopped garlic
½ tsp. dried oregano
¼ tsp. dried basil
⅛ tsp. pepper
1 lb. seafood, such as a firm fish (cod, halibut) cut in bite-size pieces, scallops, and/or shelled and deveined shrimp
4 oz. grated part-skim mozzarella cheese

Preheat oven to 400 degrees. Prepare noodles according to package directions, omitting salt and oil. Drain. Mix cornstarch with ¼ cup of the juice from the tomatoes. In a 3-quart saucepan, add cornstarch mixture with the canned tomatoes, garlic and seasonings. Simmer for 10 minutes, stirring constantly until thickened. Add seafood and simmer until seafood is cooked, but <u>do not over cook</u>.

Spray a 9" x 13" pan with non-stick cooking spray. Spread drained noodles in the pan and top with the seafood sauce. Bake for 10 minutes. Sprinkle cheese on top and return to oven until cheese is melted.

Yield: 6 servings
One serving: ¹/₆ recipe
Per serving: 301 calories, 38 grams carbohydrate, 26 grams protein, 5 grams fat
Exchanges**: 2 starch, 3 lean meat, 1 vegetable

*Sodium is figured for salt-free.

**Due to the low fat content of fish, calories are less than the exchanges would compute.

Szechuan Seafood

Serve this Chinese dish with rice or low-fat Ramen noodles. If you like spicy-hot dishes, use the larger amount of Szechuan sauce.

1 lb. seafood, such as a firm fish (cod, halibut) cut in bite-size pieces, scallops, and/or shelled and deveined shrimp
¼ cup teriyaki sauce
1 cup sliced red bell pepper
1 cup sliced green bell pepper
2 tsp. chopped garlic
16 green onions, cut into 1-inch pieces
2-4 Tbl. Szechuan sauce
⅓ cup dry roasted peanuts, unsalted

Combine seafood with teriyaki sauce, and marinate at least 1 hour in the refrigerator. Drain and discard marinade. Spray a large skillet with non-stick cooking spray and stir-fry peppers, garlic, and onion until done. Remove from skillet and keep warm.

Add one tablespoon of water to the skillet. Add seafood and cook until done, being careful when turning fish to prevent flaking. Add more water if seafood starts to stick. Return vegetables to skillet. Add remaining ingredients and heat thoroughly.

Yield: 6 cups (4 servings)
One serving: 1 ½ cups
Per serving: 211 calories, 9 grams carbohydrate, 28 grams protein, 7 grams fat
Exchanges*: ½ starch, 3 ½ lean meat, 1 vegetable

*Due to the low fat content of fish, calories are less than the exchanges would compute.

Oriental Seafood

I make this dish with jumbo shrimp that is shelled and deveined. It is easily found in the freezer section. Scallops and halibut are also very good in this recipe.

2 cups chicken broth, fat removed*
1 Tbl. soy sauce
½ tsp. ground ginger
¼ tsp. garlic powder
3 oz. coil vermicelli (fine noodles), dry
1 onion, cut in wedges
1 red bell pepper, sliced
1 can (8 oz.) sliced water chestnuts, drained
½ cup sliced carrots
1 cup broccoli pieces
1 Tbl. cornstarch
¼ cup water
1 lb. seafood, such as a firm fish (cod, halibut) cut in bite-size pieces, scallops, and/or shelled and deveined shrimp

Add all but the last 3 ingredients to a large skillet. Bring to a boil. Reduce heat to low, cover, and simmer for 8-10 minutes or until vegetables are almost done. Mix cornstarch with water. Add to skillet and bring to a slow boil, stirring until thickened. Reduce heat, add seafood, and simmer just until seafood is cooked.

Yield: 7 cups (4 servings)
One serving: 1 ³/₄ cup
Per serving: 260 calories, 30 grams carbohydrate, 30 grams protein, 2 grams fat
Exchanges**: 1 starch, 3 lean meat, 3 vegetable

*Sodium is figured for salt-free.

**Due to the low fat content of fish, calories are less than the exchanges would compute.

Seafood Dijon Fettucini

This excellent low-fat dish will remind you of Fettucini Alfredo because it looks and tastes so creamy and rich.

¼ cup light mayonnaise
¼ cup nonfat plain yogurt
2 tsp. Dijon mustard
2 tsp. dried parsley
8 oz. egg noodles - "no yolk" type (about 6 cups dry)
1 red bell pepper, chopped
2 tsp. chopped garlic
1 lb. seafood, such as a firm fish (cod, halibut) cut in bite-size pieces, scallops, and/or shelled and deveined shrimp

Mix mayonnaise, yogurt, mustard and parsley to make the sauce. Set aside. Meanwhile, cook noodles according to package directions, omitting oil and salt. Drain. Spray a skillet with non-stick cooking spray and stir-fry the pepper and garlic until done. Remove from skillet and keep warm.

Add one tablespoon of water to the skillet. Add seafood and cook until done, being careful when turning fish to prevent flaking. Add more water if seafood starts to stick. Return vegetables to skillet. Pour sauce over all and cook on low until heated. Add the noodles and toss to coat.

Yield: 7 cups (5 servings)
One serving: 1 ⅓ cups
Per serving: 300 calories, 37 grams carbohydrate, 25 grams protein, 6 grams fat
Exchanges*: 2 ½ starch, 2 ½ lean meat

Variation: Chicken Dijon Fettucini - In place of seafood, substitute 1 lb. of skinless, boneless chicken breasts, cut in bite-size pieces.

*Due to the low fat content of fish, calories are less than the exchanges would compute.

Pasta with Clam Sauce

This is an attractive way to serve pasta and will appeal to seafood and pasta lovers. Mussels can be substituted for clams.

1 lb. fresh steamer clams (about 30 small clams)
1 medium onion, chopped
1 can (28 oz.) stewed tomatoes, not drained*
1 Tbl. dried parsley
1 ½ tsp. chopped garlic
1 ½ tsp. dried marjoram
¼ tsp. salt (optional)
⅛ tsp. pepper
12 oz. angel hair pasta, dry

Wash and scrub clams. Set aside. Spray a skillet with non-stick cooking spray. Add all ingredients except clams and pasta. Simmer until onion is tender, stirring frequently. Add clams. Cover and cook until clams open, about 10 minutes. Meanwhile, cook pasta according to package directions, omitting salt and oil. Drain. Transfer to large serving bowl. Pour clams and sauce over pasta.

Yield: 6 cups pasta and 3 cups sauce (6 servings)
One serving: 1 cup of pasta and ½ cup sauce
Per serving: 278 calories, 51 grams carbohydrate, 14 grams protein, 2 grams fat
Exchanges**: 3 starch, 1 lean meat, 1 vegetable

*Sodium is figured for salt-free.

**Calories are less than what the exchanges would compute.

Oriental Pork and Noodles

This is an entire meal in one pot. It has an excellent taste and also looks appealing.

1 lb. pork tenderloin, cut in bite-size pieces
2 cups chicken broth, fat removed*
1 Tbl. soy sauce
$^{1}/_{2}$ tsp. ground ginger
$^{1}/_{4}$ tsp. garlic powder
3 oz. coil vermicelli (fine noodles), dry
1 medium onion, cut in wedges
1 red bell pepper, sliced
1 can (8 oz.) sliced water chestnuts, drained
$^{1}/_{2}$ cup sliced carrots
1 cup broccoli pieces
1 Tbl. cornstarch
$^{1}/_{4}$ cup water

Spray a skillet with non-stick cooking spray and stir-fry pork until no longer pink. Remove pork and set aside. Add broth, soy sauce, ginger, garlic powder, coil vermicelli, onion, bell pepper, water chestnuts, carrots and broccoli to the skillet. Bring to a boil. Reduce heat to low, cover, and simmer for 8 to 10 minutes or until vegetables are almost done. Mix cornstarch with water. Add to skillet. Bring to a boil, stirring until thickened. Add pork and heat thoroughly.

Yield: 7 cups (4 servings)
One serving: 1 $^{3}/_{4}$ cups
Per serving: 285 calories, 30 grams carbohydrate, 31 grams protein, 5 grams fat
Exchanges: 1 starch, 3 lean meat, 3 vegetable

*Sodium is figured for salt-free.

Spicy Pork Burritos

This simple dish will be enjoyed by anyone who likes Mexican food. Salsa can be substituted for the diced tomato.

½ green bell pepper, sliced
½ lb. pork tenderloin, cut in bite-size pieces
2 Tbl. chopped onion
1 tsp. chopped garlic
½ tsp. dried cilantro
½ tsp. dried basil
¼ tsp. cumin
½ tomato, diced
2 oz. grated reduced-fat cheddar cheese
5 flour tortillas (7 ½" diameter)

Preheat oven to 350 degrees. Spray skillet with non-stick cooking spray. Over medium heat, sauté bell pepper, pork, onion, garlic, cilantro, basil and cumin until pork is cooked. Mix in tomatoes and cheese. Spoon filling onto each tortilla. Roll tightly, and place seam side down in an 8" x 8" baking dish that has been sprayed with non-stick cooking spray. Bake 15 minutes or until heated throughout.

Yield: 5 servings
One serving: 1 filled tortilla
Per serving: 209 calories, 22 grams carbohydrate, 16 grams protein, 6 grams fat
Exchanges: 1 ½ starch, 2 lean meat

Pork with Apples and Grapes

Fresh fruit adds a sweetness to this dish that will delight anyone's palate. Serve with rice or noodles.

1 lb. pork tenderloin, cut into ½" cubes
2 small apples, cut in bite-size pieces
½ cup apple cider
1 Tbl. brown sugar (or the equivalent in artificial sweetener)
½ tsp. allspice
¼ tsp. cinnamon
1 Tbl. cornstarch
1 Tbl. water
2 cups red seedless grapes

Spray a skillet with non-stick cooking spray. Stir-fry pork until browned. Add apples, cider, sugar, allspice and cinnamon. Cover and simmer for 5 minutes or until meat is tender. Meanwhile, mix cornstarch with water and stir into meat mixture. Simmer, stirring constantly, until thickened. Add grapes and cook for 1-2 minutes until grapes are heated.

Yield: 5 cups (5 servings)
One serving: 1 cup
Per serving: 195 calories, 22 grams carbohydrate, 19 grams protein, 3 grams fat
Exchanges: 2 ½ lean meat, 1 ½ fruit

Sweet and Sour Pork

Serve this with rice or noodles and you have a complete meal.

1 lb. pork tenderloin, cut in ½" cubes
1 tsp. chopped garlic
1 cup chicken broth, fat removed*
1 tsp. soy sauce
1 green bell pepper, cut in strips
2 cups sliced celery
1 can (8 oz.) unsweetened pineapple tidbits, packed in juice
2 Tbl. cornstarch
reserved pineapple juice

Spray a skillet with non-stick cooking spray. Brown pork with garlic. Add chicken broth, soy sauce, green pepper and celery. Cover and simmer for 10 minutes. Meanwhile, drain the pineapple, reserving the juice. Blend cornstarch with reserved pineapple juice and add to the skillet. Cook, stirring constantly, until mixture thickens. Add pineapple and heat thoroughly.

Yield: 4 cups (4 servings)
One serving: 1 cup
Per serving: 212 calories, 18 grams carbohydrate, 26 grams protein, 4 grams fat
Exchanges**: 3 lean meat, 1 fruit, 1 vegetable

*Sodium is figured for salt-free.

**Due to the low fat content of the pork used, calories are less than the exchanges would compute.

Ground Meat & Sausage

When buying ground beef, look for packages labeled 9% fat, and when buying ground turkey, look for packages labeled 7% fat. If you have trouble finding these, talk to your butcher. Both ground beef and ground turkey work well in the recipes in this section. You'll find additional recipes for ground meat in the *Salads* and *Soups and Stews* sections.

The *Exchanges* listed are for either beef or turkey. However, turkey does have less saturated fat than beef. Refer to the *Nutrient Analysis of Recipes* in the back of the book for the specific nutrient differences.

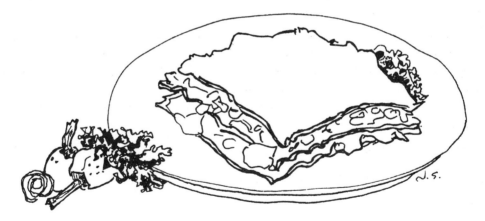

Italian Baked Ziti

This simple casserole resembles lasagna without all of the layering. Serve with a tossed salad and French bread.

8 oz. ziti pasta - tube shape (about 3 cups dry)
½ lb. extra lean ground beef (9% fat) or ground turkey (7% fat)
3 cups spaghetti sauce (less than 4g fat per 4 oz.)
2 cups low-fat cottage cheese
2 Tbl. grated Parmesan cheese
¼ cup egg substitute (equal to 1 egg)
1 tsp. dried parsley
¼ tsp. garlic powder

Preheat oven to 350 degrees. Cook ziti according to package directions, omitting salt and oil. Drain and set aside. Meanwhile, crumble meat in a large skillet sprayed with non-stick cooking spray. Sauté until meat is cooked, stirring frequently. Add spaghetti sauce.

Meanwhile, combine cottage cheese, Parmesan cheese, egg substitute, parsley, and garlic powder and mix thoroughly. Add ziti and mix well. Spread 1 cup of spaghetti sauce mixture in bottom of 9" x 13" pan that has been sprayed with non-stick cooking spray. Spoon ziti and cheese mixture into lasagna pan. Pour remaining sauce over ziti and cheese. Cover with aluminum foil and bake 30 minutes.

Yield: 8 cups (8 servings)
One serving: 1 cup
Per serving: 245 calories, 30 grams carbohydrate, 19 grams protein, 5 grams fat
Exchanges: 1 ½ starch, 2 lean meat, 1 vegetable

Pasta Sea Shell Casserole

The simplicity of this recipe makes it popular for the working mother. Children and adults alike will enjoy this casserole.

8 oz. medium-size sea shell pasta (about 4 cups dry)
3/4 lb. extra lean ground beef (9% fat) or ground turkey (7% fat)
2 tsp. chopped garlic
1/2 tsp. onion powder
3 cups spaghetti sauce (less than 4g fat per 4 oz)
1 Tbl. grated Parmesan cheese (optional)

Prepare pasta according to package directions, omitting salt and oil. Drain and set aside. Meanwhile, continue with either method below.

Stove Top: In a skillet that has been sprayed with non-stick cooking spray, brown meat with garlic and onion powder. Simmer until cooked. Add sauce and heat thoroughly. Add noodles and continue to cook until thoroughly heated. Serve with Parmesan cheese (optional).

Microwave Oven: In a 3-quart microwave-safe casserole that has been sprayed with non-stick cooking spray, cook meat with garlic and onion powder on high for 3-4 minutes, stirring after each minute to separate the meat. Add sauce, cover, and continue to cook for 3 minutes, stirring halfway through the cooking time. Mix in noodles. Cover and cook another minute or until thoroughly heated. Serve with Parmesan cheese (optional).

Yield: 8 cups (6 servings)
One serving: 1 1/3 cups
Per serving: 297 calories, 39 grams carbohydrate, 17 grams protein, 8 grams fat
Exchanges: 2 starch, 1 medium-fat meat, 2 vegetable, 1/2 fat

Sausage and Egg Casserole

This can be assembled just before cooking or it can be assembled the day before and refrigerated overnight so it is ready to pop in the oven the next morning. Because of the higher sodium content, this recipe should be limited by those on a low-sodium diet.

3 slices whole wheat bread
½ lb. turkey smoked sausage (Polish kielbasa type, 90% fat-free), chopped
2 oz. grated part-skim mozzarella cheese
2 oz. grated reduced-fat cheddar cheese
¼ cup sliced green onion or 2 Tbl. chopped dried onion
1 ½ cups egg substitute (equal to 6 eggs)
1 cup skim milk

Preheat oven to 350 degrees. Spray an 8" x 8" pan with non-stick cooking spray. Line pan with bread. Top with sausage, cheeses and onion. Mix eggs with milk and pour over top. Bake, uncovered, for 40 minutes or until a knife inserted in the center comes out clean.

Yield: 6 servings
One serving: ⅙ recipe
Per serving: 186 calories, 12 grams carbohydrate, 20 grams protein, 6 grams fat
Exchanges: ½ milk, ½ starch, 2 lean meat

Note: For 12 servings, double this recipe and bake in a 9" x 13" pan for 1 hour.

South of the Border Lasagna

This dish looks great, tastes delicious and is highly recommended for entertaining.

1 lb. extra lean ground beef (9% fat) or ground turkey (7% fat)
1 can (16 oz.) diced tomatoes, not drained*
1 can (7 oz.) diced green chiles
2 tsp. chili powder
1 $\frac{1}{2}$ tsp. cumin
$\frac{1}{2}$ tsp. pepper
$\frac{1}{4}$ tsp. garlic powder
$\frac{1}{8}$ tsp. cayenne pepper
$\frac{1}{4}$ cup egg substitute (equal to 1 egg)
2 cups low-fat cottage cheese
1 oz. grated part-skim mozzarella cheese
14 corn tortillas
1 can (17 oz.) whole kernel corn, drained*
2 cups shredded lettuce
1 cup chopped fresh tomatoes
4 green onions, chopped
1 oz. grated reduced-fat cheddar cheese

Preheat oven to 350 degrees. Brown meat in a skillet that has been sprayed with non-stick cooking spray. Add canned tomatoes, chiles and seasonings and set aside. In a small bowl, combine egg substitute, cottage cheese and mozzarella cheese.

Spray a 9" x 13" pan with non-stick cooking spray. Cover bottom and sides of pan with 6 tortillas. Layer in this order: 1 can of corn, $\frac{1}{2}$ meat mixture, 4 tortillas, $\frac{1}{2}$ meat mixture, 4 tortillas, cheese mixture. Bake for 30 minutes or until bubbly. Remove from oven and top with remaining ingredients. Serve immediately.

Yield: 8 servings
One serving: $\frac{1}{8}$ recipe
Per serving: 332 calories, 35 grams carbohydrate, 25 grams protein, 10 grams fat
Exchanges: 2 starch, 2 medium-fat meat, 1 vegetable

*Sodium is figured for salt-free.

Cornbread Casserole

You'll find this to be a meal that the whole family will enjoy. Corn can be substituted for the mixed vegetables.

2 cups frozen mixed vegetables
1 lb. extra lean ground beef (9% fat) or ground turkey (7% fat)
1 medium onion, chopped
1 cup beef broth, fat removed*
2 Tbl. unbleached flour
1 tsp. chili powder
¼ tsp. salt (optional)
⅛ tsp. pepper

Cornbread Topping:
½ cup yellow cornmeal
½ cup unbleached flour
2 Tbl. sugar
2 tsp. baking powder
¼ tsp. salt (optional)
2 Tbl. canola oil
¼ cup egg substitute (equal to 1 egg)
½ cup skim milk

Preheat oven to 350 degrees. Cook frozen vegetables according to package directions, omitting salt. Drain any liquid and set aside. In a skillet that has been sprayed with non-stick cooking spray, brown meat and onion.

Meanwhile, combine flour with broth in a covered container and shake well to prevent lumps. Add to meat mixture along with the chili powder, pepper and salt (optional). Bring to a boil, stirring constantly, until thickened. Add cooked vegetables and mix well.

Pour into an 8″ x 8″ pan that has been sprayed with non-stick cooking spray. Meanwhile, in a medium bowl, combine the dry ingredients for the cornbread topping. Add liquid ingredients and mix just until blended. Spread over meat mixture and bake for 30-35 minutes or until cornbread is golden brown.

Yield: 6 servings
One serving: $^1/_6$ recipe
Per serving: 355 calories, 35 grams carbohydrate, 21 grams protein, 14 grams fat
Exchanges: 2 starch, 2 medium-fat meat, 1 vegetable, $^1/_2$ fat

*Sodium is figured for salt-free.

Pasta Olé

This is good served hot and we surprised ourselves to find that we also liked it served cold. So keep this in mind for the hot summer months.

6 oz. angel hair pasta, dry
$^1/_2$ lb. extra lean ground beef (9% fat) or ground turkey (7% fat)
1 tsp. chili powder
$^1/_2$ tsp. paprika
$^1/_2$ tsp. garlic powder
$^1/_2$ cup salsa, thick and chunky
1 $^1/_2$ cups shredded lettuce
2 oz. grated reduced-fat cheddar cheese

Cook noodles according to package directions, omitting salt and oil. Drain. Brown meat in a skillet that has been sprayed with non-stick cooking spray. Add seasonings to meat and mix well. Arrange hot noodles on a heated platter and top with seasoned meat. Spoon salsa over meat and top with shredded lettuce and grated cheese. Serve immediately.

Yield: 4 servings
One serving: $^1/_4$ recipe
Per serving: 315 calories, 35 grams carbohydrate, 21 grams protein, 10 grams fat
Exchanges: 2 starch, 2 medium-fat meat, 1 vegetable

Sour Cream Enchiladas

This is a family favorite. Serve with salsa and a tossed green salad. The variation, Turkey Enchiladas, listed below is great for using leftover turkey. This recipe can be assembled a day ahead of time and refrigerated until ready to cook. Increase cooking time to 30 minutes.

⅓ **cup unbleached flour**
1 cup skim milk
1 ½ cups chicken or beef broth, fat removed*
1 lb. extra lean ground beef (9% fat) or ground turkey (7% fat)
1 ½ tsp. cumin
½ tsp. chili powder
¼ tsp. salt (optional)
1 can (7 oz.) diced green chiles
½ cup chopped green onion
1 cup nonfat sour cream
8 flour tortillas (7 ½″ diameter)
4 oz. grated reduced-fat cheddar cheese

Preheat oven to 350 degrees. To make the sauce, combine flour with milk in a covered container and shake well to prevent lumps. Pour into a 4-cup glass measure and add the broth. Heat on high in the microwave for 6-8 minutes, stirring every 60 seconds until bubbly and thickened. Meanwhile, brown meat in a skillet that has been sprayed with non-stick cooking spray. Add one half of the sauce to the ground meat with the seasonings, chiles, green onion and sour cream.

Spray a 9″ x 13″ pan with non-stick cooking spray. Spread each tortilla with ½ cup of meat sauce and a tablespoon of cheese. Roll and place in pan seam side down. Repeat until all the tortillas are filled. Pour the remaining sauce and any remaining meat mixture over the filled tortillas, being sure that all are covered with sauce. Bake for 20 minutes. Sprinkle with cheese and return to the oven for 10 minutes.

Yield: 8 servings
One serving: ¹/₈ recipe
Per serving: 308 calories, 29 grams carbohydrate, 21 grams protein, 12 grams fat
Exchanges: 2 starch, 2 medium-fat meat

Variation: Turkey Enchiladas - Replace ground meat with 2 cups of cooked, cubed turkey or chicken. Omit the step for browning the meat.
Per serving: 256 calories, 29 grams carbohydrate, 21 grams protein, 6 grams fat
Exchanges: 2 starch, 2 lean meat

*Sodium is figured for salt-free.

Sweet and Sour Beans

Here's a recipe that can be served as a main dish or as a side dish. It is especially good for July 4th parties and will be a favorite for all ages.

¹/₂ lb. extra lean ground beef (9% fat) or ground turkey (7% fat)
1 medium onion, diced
2 cans (16 oz. each) vegetarian baked beans, drained
1 can (8 oz.) tomato sauce*
2 tsp. chopped garlic
1 tsp. Worcestershire sauce
1 tsp. chili powder
¹/₂ tsp. dry mustard
dash of Tabasco sauce
1 can (8 oz.) pineapple tidbits in juice, drained

Spray a skillet with non-stick cooking spray. Brown meat and onion. Add remaining ingredients and simmer, uncovered, for 10 minutes.

Yield: 4 ¹/₂ cups (9 servings)
One serving: ¹/₂ cup
Per serving: 154 calories, 21 grams carbohydrate, 9 grams protein, 3 grams fat
Exchanges: 1 starch, 1 lean meat, ¹/₂ fruit

*Sodium is figured for salt-free.

Unstuffed Cabbage Casserole

If you're looking for a quick one-dish meal, try this one on a busy day. This is a simple version of traditional stuffed cabbage rolls.

1 small head of cabbage (about 1 ½ lbs.)
1 cup boiling water
1 cup quick-cooking brown rice, uncooked
½ lb. extra lean ground beef (9% fat) or ground turkey (7% fat)
1 tsp. chopped garlic
¼ tsp. salt (optional)
1 can (10 ¾ oz.) tomato soup
½ can water

Preheat oven to 350 degrees. Slice cabbage. In a skillet that has been sprayed with non–stick cooking spray, stir-fry cabbage until limp. Meanwhile, spray a 2-quart covered casserole with non-stick cooking spray. Add 1 cup of boiling water and rice to the casserole. Cover while preparing the rest of the ingredients.

Add the cabbage to the casserole. Brown meat with garlic and salt (optional) in the same skillet used to stir-fry the cabbage. Spread over cabbage. Mix soup with water. Pour over all and gently stir to mix. Cover and bake for 55 minutes or until rice is cooked and cabbage is tender.

Yield: 7 cups (4 servings)
One serving: 1 ¾ cups
Per serving: 291 calories, 37 grams carbohydrate, 15 grams protein, 9 grams fat
Exchanges: 2 starch, 1 medium-fat meat, 1 vegetable, ½ fat

Desserts

Think of desserts as extras. If you are trying to limit calories, concentrate on other foods that will provide more vitamins and minerals. The recipes in this section are lower in calories and fat than most desserts but should still be used in moderation.

Sugar is used in some of the recipes and these recipes may be used by people with diabetes. However, these foods should be substituted for other carbohydrates and not simply added to the meal.

Apple Crisp Parfait

This version of apple crisp takes on a new appearance with a light, flavorful topping.

3 cups sliced & peeled apples (about 3 medium apples)
1/3 cup old fashioned cooking oats
3 Tbl. brown sugar (or the equivalent in artificial sweetener)
2 Tbl. water
1 tsp. cinnamon

Topping:
4 oz. nonfat vanilla yogurt (sweetened with artificial sweetener)
1/4 tsp. cinnamon
1/8 tsp. nutmeg
3/4 cup light whipped topping

Mix apples with oats, brown sugar, water and cinnamon. Cook according to microwave or oven method below.

Microwave Oven: Place apples in a 1-quart microwave-safe bowl. Cover with wax paper and microwave on high for 5 to 7 minutes, rotating 1/4 turn halfway through cooking time. Depending on thickness of fruit, cooking time may be longer.

Conventional Oven: Place apples in a 1-quart casserole. Bake at 350 degrees for 25 minutes.

Topping: Mix yogurt with seasonings. Fold whipped topping into yogurt. Serve a dollop of topping over hot or chilled apple crisp.

Yield: 2 cups apples and 1 cup topping (4 servings)
One serving: 1/2 cup apples and 1/4 cup topping
Per serving: 167 calories, 34 grams carbohydrate, 2 grams protein, 2 grams fat
Exchanges: 1 starch, 1 fruit

Baked Grapenut Pudding

This is a low-fat version of a very popular New England dessert. If you like custard, you'll like this. Plan on making this when you're using the oven for a casserole or stew.

1/2 **cup Grapenut cereal**
2 1/2 **cups warm skim milk**
1/2 **cup egg substitute (equal to 2 eggs)**
1/3 **cup sugar (or the equivalent in artificial sweetener)**
1 **tsp. vanilla**
1/8 **tsp. salt (optional)**
nutmeg

Preheat oven to 350 degrees. Mix all of the ingredients except nutmeg. Pour into an oven-proof 1-quart baking dish that has been sprayed with non-stick cooking spray. Sprinkle with nutmeg. Bake for one hour.

Yield: 3 cups (6 servings)
One serving: 1/2 cup
Per serving: 126 calories, 24 grams carbohydrate, 6 grams protein, 0 grams fat
Exchanges: 1/2 milk, 1 starch

Raisin Bread Pudding

This is a great dessert topped with light whipped topping. Also think about having this for breakfast with fresh fruit.

7 slices of whole wheat bread, cut in cubes (about 4 cups)
½ cup seedless raisins
2 cups skim milk
¾ cup egg substitute (equal to 3 eggs)
⅓ cup sugar (or the equivalent in artificial sweetener)
2 tsp. vanilla extract
½ tsp. cinnamon
½ tsp. nutmeg
⅛ tsp. salt (optional)

Preheat oven to 350 degrees. Place bread cubes in an 8″ x 8″ pan that has been sprayed with non-stick cooking spray. Mix remaining ingredients and pour over bread cubes. Bake for 40 minutes or until a sharp knife inserted in the center comes out clean.

Yield: 9 servings
One serving: ⅑ recipe
Per serving: 141 calories, 27 grams carbohydrate, 6 grams protein, 1 gram fat
Exchanges: ½ milk, 1 starch, ½ fruit

Variation: Applesauce Bread Pudding – Reduce milk to 1 cup and substitute 1 cup unsweetened applesauce for the raisins.
Per serving: 118 calories, 22 grams carbohydrate, 5 grams protein, 1 gram fat
Exchanges: 1 ½ starch

Peach Custard

This is a great recipe that uses ripe peaches. Try this for dessert with a dollop of light whipped topping or serve for breakfast either cold, or heated in the microwave.

5 peeled and sliced fresh peaches (about 5 cups)
1 cup egg substitute (equal to 4 eggs)
1 tsp. lemon juice
1 tsp. vanilla extract
$\frac{1}{2}$ cup sugar (or the equivalent in artificial sweetener)
$\frac{1}{8}$ tsp. salt (optional)
$\frac{1}{4}$ cup unbleached flour
$\frac{1}{8}$ tsp. cinnamon

Preheat oven to 350 degrees. Spread fruit in an 8″ x 8″ pan that has been sprayed with non-stick cooking spray. Mix egg substitute, lemon juice and vanilla extract with an electric mixer or wire whisk. Mix in sugar and salt (optional). Gradually add the flour while whipping to prevent lumps. Pour over fruit. Sprinkle with cinnamon. Bake for 45 minutes or until a knife inserted in the center comes out clean.

Yield: 9 servings
One serving: $\frac{1}{9}$ of recipe
Per serving: 133 calories, 29 grams carbohydrate, 4 grams protein, 0 grams fat
Exchanges: $\frac{1}{2}$ lean meat, 2 fruit

Variation: Pear Custard - Substitute fresh pears and mace for the peaches and cinnamon.

Baked Pears with Chocolate Sauce

This is a very attractive dessert that is also delicious. The uniqueness of a pear, including the stem, drizzled with chocolate sauce appeals to all ages. Use pears that are ripe but not too soft.

4 small pears with stem intact
2 Tbl. orange juice
4 tsp. nonfat chocolate sauce (such as Hershey's)

Peel pears. Partially core from bottom leaving the stem intact. If necessary, take a small slice off the bottom to make it flat so the pear can stand without tipping. Pour orange juice onto a plate and roll the pears in the juice to coat. This will prevent browning. Arrange pears in a covered 2-quart microwave-safe casserole. Microwave on high for 3 minutes, rotating 1/4 turn halfway through cooking time. Let sit 5 minutes. Cool in refrigerator until chilled. To serve, place a pear on a plate with the stem up and drizzle with chocolate sauce.

Yield: 4 servings
One serving: 1 pear
Per serving: 130 calories, 30 grams carbohydrate, 1 gram protein, 1 gram fat
Exchanges: 2 fruit

Glazed Fruit Cup

This looks especially attractive in parfait glasses or even wine glasses. It can also be served over angel food cake or pudding.

¼ cup sugar-free jam or jelly (spreadable fruit)
4 cups fresh fruit, any combination of berries, grapes, or sliced peaches

Melt jelly in the microwave on high for about 15 minutes. Cool to room temperature, about 15 minutes. Pour over fruit and gently toss to coat.

Yield: 4 cups (4 servings)
One serving: 1 cup
Per serving: 111 calories, 26 grams carbohydrate, 1 gram protein, 0 grams fat
Exchanges: 2 fruit

Strawberry Yogurt Mousse

Serve this light dessert in parfait glasses with a fresh strawberry sitting on top of a dollop of light whipped topping.

1 ½ cups light whipped topping
8 oz. nonfat strawberry yogurt (sweetened with artificial sweetener)
2 cups sliced strawberries

Fold whipped topping into yogurt. Add strawberries and chill.

Yield: 4 cups (8 servings)
One serving: ½ cup
Per serving: 49 calories, 7 grams carbohydrate, 1 gram protein, 2 grams fat
Exchanges: ½ fruit, ½ fat

Chocolate Peanut Butter Frozen Bars

Kids will enjoy these bars for an after-school snack or a summer treat. And it's easy enough for kids to make, especially if they are using instant pudding. This recipe works well with instant or cooked pudding.

2 packages (1.3 oz. each) sugar-free chocolate pudding (instant or cook type)
3 ⅓ cups skim milk
¼ cup peanut butter
27 graham cracker squares (2 ½")

Mix pudding according to package directions, except use 3 ⅓ cups of milk. Beat in peanut butter. Line a 9" x 13" pan with half the graham cracker squares. Three squares will have to be cut in half to line the pan. Spread pudding mixture over graham crackers. Top with remaining crackers. Freeze for four hours. Cut into squares and remove from pan. Store in a plastic bag in the freezer.

Yield: 13 ½ bars (13 ½ servings)
One serving: 1 bar
Per serving: 124 calories, 18 grams carbohydrate, 5 grams protein, 4 grams fat
Exchanges: 1 starch, 1 fat

Popsicles

You can vary the flavor of the gelatin and the Kool-Aid to please different flavor preferences.

1 pkg. (0.3 oz.) artificially sweetened cherry Kool-Aid
1 pkg. (0.3 oz.) sugar-free cherry-flavored gelatin
2 cups boiling water
2 cups cold water

Dissolve Kool-Aid and gelatin in boiling water. Mix in cold water. Pour into popsicle molds and freeze until firm, about 3-6 hours.

Yield: 16 popsicles
One serving: 1 popsicle
Per serving: 3 calories, 0 grams carbohydrate, 0 grams protein, 0 grams fat
Exchanges: "free"

Variation: Shaved Ice - Make popsicles as listed above except pour into a shallow container and freeze until firm (about 3-4 hours). To serve, shave ice by scraping with a spoon.

Peach Popsicles

Kids will enjoy these fruit popsicles on a hot summer day. Other canned fruit can be substituted for the peaches.

1 can (16 oz.) sliced peaches, packed in juice, not drained
2 Tbl. sugar (or the equivalent in artificial sweetener)

In a blender, blend all ingredients until smooth. Pour into popsicle containers or a shallow pan (for shaved ice) and freeze until firm, about 3-5 hours.

Yield: 8 popsicles
One serving: 1 popsicle
Per serving: 40 calories, 10 grams carbohydrate, 0 grams protein, 0 grams fat
Exchanges: 1/2 fruit

Mandarin Yogurt Delight

The orange color makes this an attractive dessert. Serve in sherbet dishes with a dollop of light whipped topping. This also works well as a fruit salad.

1 pkg. (0.3 oz.) sugar-free orange-flavored gelatin
¾ cup boiling water
8 oz. nonfat vanilla yogurt (sweetened with artificial sweetener)
1 can (11 oz.) mandarin oranges, drained

Dissolve gelatin in boiling water. Add yogurt and stir until smooth. Chill until the consistency of egg whites, about 20 minutes. Add drained fruit. Spoon into sherbet dishes and refrigerate until set.

Yield: 2 ½ cups (5 servings)
One serving: ½ cup
Per serving: 40 calories, 7 grams carbohydrate, 3 grams protein, 0 grams fat
Exchanges: ½ fruit

Strawberry Delight

You'll enjoy the refreshing taste of this recipe as a salad or as a dessert. This is another great potluck dish and looks especially attractive.

1 pkg. (0.3 oz.) sugar-free raspberry-flavored gelatin
1 pkg. (0.3 oz.) sugar-free strawberry-flavored gelatin
1 ½ cups boiling water
1 pkg. (16 oz.) frozen unsweetened strawberries, sliced
1 can (15 ¼ oz.) pineapple tidbits (in juice), drained
2 Tbl. lemon juice
8 oz. nonfat vanilla yogurt (sweetened with artificial sweetener)

Dissolve gelatin in boiling water. Add strawberries and stir until thawed. Stir in drained pineapple and lemon juice. Pour half into an 8" x 8" glass pan and refrigerate. Refrigerate the remaining half until the consistency of egg whites. After about 20 minutes, spread yogurt over the mixture in the 8" x 8" pan. Top with the remaining mixture that is partially set. Chill until firm.

Yield: about 5 cups (7 servings)
One serving: about ¾ cup
Per serving: 60 calories, 12 grams carbohydrate, 2 grams protein, 0 grams fat
Exchanges: 1 fruit

Strawberry-Pineapple Shortcake

You can have shortcake year-round with this recipe.

1 pkg. (0.3 oz.) sugar-free strawberry-flavored gelatin
³/₄ cups boiling water
1 package (8 oz.) frozen unsweetened strawberries, sliced
1 can (15 ¹/₄ oz.) crushed pineapple (in juice), not drained
1 Tbl. lemon juice
8 slices of angel food cake (about 1 ounce each)

Dissolve gelatin in boiling water. Add strawberries and stir until thawed. Stir in undrained pineapple and lemon juice. Chill.

Top cake slices with chilled sauce.

Yield: 8 cake slices and 4 cups of sauce (8 servings)
One serving: 1 slice of cake and ¹/₂ cup strawberry sauce
Per serving: 113 calories, 25 grams carbohydrate, 2 grams protein, 0 grams fat
Exchanges: 1 starch, ¹/₂ fruit

Banana Cream Pie

You'll find this pie to be a family favorite. I prefer the kind of pudding that you cook instead of the instant because I feel it has a better flavor and texture.

1 small package (0.8 oz.) sugar-free vanilla pudding (cook type)
1 ²/₃ cups skim milk
4 oz. nonfat vanilla yogurt (sweetened with artificial sweetener)
26 vanilla wafers
2 bananas, about 7″ each, sliced (about 2 cups)
1 cup light whipped topping

Prepare pudding according to package directions, except use only 1 ²/₃ cups of milk. Cool slightly before adding the yogurt. Line the bottom of an 8″ pie pan with 12 vanilla wafers (not crushed). Arrange banana slices over the vanilla wafers. Place remaining 14 vanilla wafers standing up around the rim of the pan. Pour in cooled pudding. Top with light whipped topping. Refrigerate for two hours before serving so the pudding will be firm. When serving, cut each piece to include two of the stand up vanilla wafers.

Yield: 7 servings
One serving: ¹/₇ pie
Per serving: 160 calories, 28 grams carbohydrate, 4 grams protein, 4 grams fat
Exchanges: ¹/₂ milk, 1 starch, ¹/₂ fruit

Chocolate Cream Pie

A chocolate lovers dream. It's almost too good to be true, yet so low in fat and sugar! I prefer the kind of pudding that you cook instead of the instant as I like the flavor and texture better.

2 packages (1.3 oz. each) sugar-free chocolate pudding (cook type)
3 ¹/₃ cups skim milk
33 vanilla wafers
1 cup light whipped topping

Prepare pudding according to package directions, except use only 3 ¹/₃ cups of milk. Line the bottom of a 9″ pie pan with 17 vanilla wafers (not crushed). Place remaining 16 vanilla wafers standing up around the rim of the pan. Pour in pudding. Top with light whipped topping. Refrigerate for two hours before serving so the pudding will be firm. When serving, cut each piece to include two of the stand up vanilla wafers.

Yield: 8 servings
One serving: ¹/₈ pie
Per serving: 159 calories, 26 grams carbohydrate, 5 grams protein, 4 grams fat
Exchanges: ¹/₂ milk, 1 starch, 1 fat

Variation: Chocolate Peanut Butter Pie - Add ¹/₄ cup of peanut butter to the pudding. This can be served as a refrigerator dessert or frozen (allow 4-5 hours to freeze).
Per serving: 209 calories, 28 grams carbohydrate, 7 grams protein, 8 grams fat
Exchanges: ¹/₂ milk, 1 ¹/₂ starch, 1 fat

Chocolate Vanilla Swirl Pie

You'll find this pie to be a family favorite. I prefer to use the kind of pudding you cook instead of the instant as I like the texture and flavor better.

1 small package (1.3 oz.) sugar-free chocolate pudding (cook type)
1 ²/₃ cups skim milk
¼ cup peanut butter
1 small package (0.8 oz.) sugar-free vanilla pudding (cook type)
1 ²/₃ cups skim milk
33 vanilla wafers

Prepare chocolate pudding according to package directions, except use only 1 ²/₃ cups of milk. Beat in peanut butter and set aside. Prepare vanilla pudding according to package directions, except use only 1 ²/₃ cups of milk. Line the bottom of an 9″ pie pan with 17 vanilla wafers (not crushed). Place remaining 16 vanilla wafers standing up around the rim of the pan. Pour in cooled chocolate pudding. Drop in spoonfuls of the vanilla pudding, swirling into the chocolate pudding with the back of a spoon.

Refrigerate for two hours before serving so the pudding will be firm. When serving, cut each piece to include two of the stand up vanilla wafers.

Yield: 8 servings
One serving: ¹/₈ pie
Per serving: 187 calories, 25 grams carbohydrate, 7 grams protein, 7 grams fat
Exchanges: ¹/₂ milk, 1 starch, 1 fat

New York Cheesecake

Yes, this is a no-fat cheesecake and yes, it tastes great. Our home economist, Claudia Schon, tested this recipe no less than a dozen times to get it just right. Sliced fruit such as kiwi, blueberries and strawberries can be attractively arranged on top to make this dessert look especially appealing. Or you can substitute canned reduced-calorie cherry pie filling for the fresh fruit.

24 oz. nonfat cream cheese (bar type) at room temperature
½ cup sugar
½ tsp. vanilla extract
½ tsp. almond extract
¾ cup egg substitute (equal to 3 eggs)
2 Tbl. packaged cornflake crumbs (optional)
2 cups fresh fruit, sliced

Preheat oven to 325 degrees. In a large bowl combine cream cheese, sugar, vanilla and almond extract. Using an electric mixer, beat at high speed until blended. On low speed, beat in egg substitute. Increase speed to high and continue to beat until well blended.

Spray a 9" pie pan with non-stick cooking spray. Add cornflake crumbs (optional) to the pan and shake lightly to coat bottom and sides with crumbs. Pour in cream cheese mixture. Bake for 45 minutes or until center is set but not firm. Cool on wire rack. Arrange fresh fruit on top of cheesecake before serving. This dessert should be stored in the refrigerator several hours before serving.

Yield: 12 servings
One serving: ¹/₁₂ cheesecake
Per serving: 94 calories, 14 grams carbohydrate, 9 grams protein, 0 grams fat
Exchanges: 1 skim milk

Variation: Double this recipe for a 9" spring form pan and bake for 1 hour and 35 minutes. Makes 24 servings. One serving is equivalent to the same nutritional value as for 1 serving listed above.

Pumpkin Cheesecake

Serve this low-fat cheesecake during the holiday season. The top will crack so plan on serving with a dollop of light whipped topping to hide the cracks.

24 oz. nonfat cream cheese (bar type) at room temperature
¾ cup canned pumpkin
½ cup sugar
1 tsp. vanilla extract
¾ cup egg substitute (equal to 3 eggs)
½ tsp. cinnamon
¼ tsp. ground cloves
2 Tbl. packaged cornflake crumbs (optional)

Preheat oven to 325 degrees. In a large bowl combine cream cheese, pumpkin, sugar and vanilla. Using an electric mixer, beat at high speed until blended. On low speed, beat in egg substitute and spices. Increase speed to high and continue to beat until well blended.

Spray a 9″ pie pan with non-stick cooking spray. Add cornflake crumbs (optional) to the pan and shake lightly to coat bottom and sides with crumbs. Pour in cream cheese mixture. Bake for 45 minutes or until center is set but not firm. Cool on wire rack. This dessert should be stored in the refrigerator several hours before serving.

Yield: 12 servings
One serving: ¹/₁₂ cheesecake
Per serving: 86 calories, 12 grams carbohydrate, 9 grams protein, 0 grams fat
Exchanges: 1 skim milk

Nutrient Analysis of Recipes

	Amount	Calories	Protein (grams)	Carbo-hydrate (grams)	Fat (grams)	Choles-terol (mg)	Saturated Fat (grams)	Dietary Fiber (grams)	Calcium (mg)	Iron (mg)	Sodium (mg)	Potas-sium (mg)	Phos-phorus (mg)
APPETIZERS AND SAUCES													
Bean & Cheese Dip	2 Tbl.	39	2.0	5.0	1.2	2.5	0.7	0.6	16	0.5	166	102	4.7
Bean & Salsa Dip	2 Tbl.	24	1.2	4.7	0.0	0.0	0.0	0.6	6	0.4	143	94	0.0
Cheese Sauce	2 Tbl.	40	3.6	3.3	1.3	5.6	0.8	0.0	102	0.1	72	58	68.9
Chili Cheese Dip	2 Tbl.	40	2.8	3.3	1.7	7.4	1.0	0.4	19	0.5	147	8	4.7
Cottage Cheese Bkd Potato Topping	2 Tbl.	18	2.9	1.0	0.2	1.0	0.1	0.0	23	0.0	89	33	35.8
Cream Cheese Spread	1 Tbl.	13	1.5	0.9	0.3	3.2	0.0	0.0	42	0.1	60	7	1.2
Cucumber Spread	2 Tbl.	13	2.1	0.9	0.1	3.1	0.0	0.0	54	0.1	86	14	1.9
Dijon Sauce	2 tsp.	21	0.2	1.4	1.6	0.1	0.1	0.0	7	0.0	63	10	6.3
Dill Cheese Sauce	2 Tbl.	40	3.6	3.3	1.3	5.6	0.8	0.0	102	0.1	72	58	68.9
Herbed Cream Cheese	1 Tbl.	39	1.5	1.4	3.1	5.0	1.5	0.0	21	0.2	92	48	10.9
Layered Black Bean Dip	2 Tbl.	38	2.6	4.3	1.2	4.9	0.4	0.6	45	0.3	81	54	38.6
Pimento and Cheese Spread	1 Tbl.	34	2.3	0.8	2.4	5.1	0.8	0.0	64	0.1	81	11	39.5
Sour Cream Baked Potato Topping	2 Tbl.	22	0.9	1.7	1.3	6.4	0.0	0.0	35	0.0	16	16	7.7
Tuna Paté	2 Tbl.	34	7.0	1.0	0.2	8.2	0.0	0.0	53	0.3	176	55	33.0
Veggie Spread	2 Tbl.	28	2.1	1.7	1.4	2.5	0.1	0.2	56	0.1	119	34	5.3
BREADS													
Apple Cider Pancakes	2	144	3.7	30.4	0.8	0.0	0.1	0.0	101	1.3	368	126	204.0
Banana Bread	1/9 recipe	166	5.2	34.6	0.7	0.1	0.2	2.5	100	1.5	143	188	158.0
Biscuit Wedges	1	185	5.0	32.2	4.0	0.5	0.3	0.9	167	1.3	152	108	227.8
Bread Sticks	1	106	5.0	18.2	1.5	0.0	0.0	0.2	2	0.1	220	7	3.4
Buttermilk Bran Breakfast Squares	1/9 recipe	169	5.3	34.9	1.0	1.0	0.3	4.9	47	2.4	285	254	197.0
Carrot Muffins	1	163	3.9	35.7	0.5	0.0	0.0	0.9	29	1.2	138	104	32.8

Note: Ingredients listed as optional are not included in analysis. If a choice of ingredients is given, the first one listed is used.

	Amount	Calories	Protein (grams)	Carbohydrate (grams)	Fat (grams)	Cholesterol (mg)	Saturated Fat (grams)	Dietary Fiber (grams)	Calcium (mg)	Iron (mg)	Sodium (mg)	Potassium (mg)	Phosphorus (mg)
Date Nut Bread	1/16 recipe	156	2.8	31.8	2.0	0.0	0.1	0.8	6	0.8	86	94	13.7
Drop Biscuits	1	165	4.9	27.5	4.0	0.5	0.3	0.9	167	1.3	152	106	228.0
Focaccia Cheese Bread	1/16 recipe	87	3.9	13.0	2.1	2.6	0.5	3.2	53	1.0	212	52	92.7
Focaccia Veggie Bread	1/16 recipe	77	2.8	12.9	1.6	0.2	0.2	3.3	23	1.0	183	112	75.3
Mexican Cornbread	1/9 recipe	169	6.0	22.1	6.3	4.8	1.1	1.6	88	1.1	160	144	99.7
Pineapple Bread	1/9 recipe	158	4.7	33.3	0.6	0.0	0.1	2.3	102	1.7	179	153	150.0
Pumpkin Bread	1/9 recipe	187	5.4	39.6	0.8	0.0	0.1	3.0	40	1.9	186	145	80.1
Traditional Biscuits	1	169	5.0	28.2	4.0	0.5	0.3	0.9	167	1.3	152	108	227.8

SOUPS AND STEWS

	Amount	Calories	Protein (grams)	Carbohydrate (grams)	Fat (grams)	Cholesterol (mg)	Saturated Fat (grams)	Dietary Fiber (grams)	Calcium (mg)	Iron (mg)	Sodium (mg)	Potassium (mg)	Phosphorus (mg)
Black Bean Soup	1 1/4 cups	171	11.1	29.8	0.8	0.0	0.2	5.5	56	2.3	276	553	161.2
Chicken Chili	1 1/2 cups	296	25.8	42.0	2.8	34.5	0.5	11.9	110	4.9	80	954	341.0
Chicken Pasta Stew	1 1/2 cups	223	24.6	25.1	2.7	49.1	0.7	1.6	42	2.3	134	430	205.9
Chicken Soup	1 1/2 cups	142	15.4	17.6	1.1	17.1	0.2	2.2	30	1.6	146	502	105.1
Creamy Cabbage Soup	1 1/2 cups	121	11.3	14.6	2.0	15.0	0.5	0.4	113	1.2	282	519	103.0
Garden Minestrone Soup (beef)	1 1/2 cups	302	24.4	28.9	9.9	46.8	3.7	5.4	107	4.7	142	1001	195.0
Garden Minestrone Soup (turkey)	1 1/2 cups	285	23.6	28.9	8.3	37.8	2.2	5.4	116	4.5	148	974	212.0
Green Chile Pork Stew	1 1/2 cups	269	22.9	36.5	3.5	52.4	1.2	5.9	46	2.6	130	970	263.0
Oven Beef Stew	1 cup	220	22.9	23.2	3.9	54.7	1.3	3.4	41	3.5	87	831	247.0
Sausage and Lentil Stew	1 cup	228	13.0	39.6	1.9	13.1	0.5	1.1	58	4.1	195	756	237.6
Seafood Gumbo	1 1/2 cups	163	23.0	13.7	1.8	33.3	0.3	2.0	90	1.5	122	935	189.0
Sherried Broth	1 cup	18	4.7	2.3	0.0	0.0	0.0	0.0	2	0.1	70	207	4.0
Spiced Tomato Broth	1 cup	41	3.3	6.8	0.1	0.0	0.0	1.5	18	0.8	46	375	28.7
Tortilla Soup	1 1/4 cups	77	6.2	11.5	0.6	0.0	0.1	0.8	39	0.6	105	350	74.2
Venus De Milo Soup (beef)	1 1/2 cups	293	21.6	32.0	8.7	40.8	3.3	4.5	66	3.3	142	734	182.0
Venus De Milo Soup (turkey)	1 1/2 cups	278	20.9	32.0	7.4	33.1	2.0	4.5	74	3.1	147	710	197.0

Note: Ingredients listed as optional are not included in analysis. If a choice of ingredients is given, the first one listed is used.

	Amount	Calories	Protein (grams)	Carbo- hydrate (grams)	Fat (grams)	Choles- terol (mg)	Saturated Fat (grams)	Dietary Fiber (grams)	Calcium (mg)	Iron (mg)	Sodium (mg)	Potas- sium (mg)	Phos- phorus (mg)
VEGETABLES													
Baked Sweet Potatoes or Yams	½ potato	60	1.0	13.9	0.1	0.0	0.0	1.7	16	0.3	6	198	31.4
Barbecued Corn on the Cob	1 ear	136	3.9	28.1	0.9	0.0	0.1	2.7	4	0.8	5	316	94.5
Barbecued Potatoes	¼ recipe	126	2.6	28.7	0.1	0.0	0.0	2.8	12	1.6	9	476	64.9
Barbecued Vegetable Kabobs	¼ recipe	23	0.9	4.5	0.2	0.0	0.0	0.7	8	0.3	2	182	26.4
Barbecued Zucchini	¼ recipe	12	0.8	1.9	0.1	0.0	0.0	0.6	10	0.3	2	217	20.8
Black Bean Stuffed Peppers	⅙ recipe	160	8.5	26.0	2.5	6.8	1.1	4.1	110	1.4	129	362	157.0
Creamy Mashed Potatoes	½ cup	146	3.7	30.5	1.1	5.0	0.0	2.9	52	1.8	27	508	80.9
Cucumbers with Dill Yogurt	½ cup	35	0.8	2.7	2.4	0.1	0.2	0.0	24	0.2	56	97	23.5
Cucumbers w/ Onions and Sour Crm	½ cup	21	0.7	3.3	0.6	2.4	0.0	0.4	19	0.2	6	88	14.2
Green Bean Sauté	½ cup	27	1.1	5.2	0.1	0.0	0.0	1.5	17	0.6	2	140	31.6
Grilled Eggplant	¼ recipe	62	1.8	7.1	2.9	1.2	0.6	0.0	30	0.3	32	250	38.3
Grilled Vegetable Medley	¼ recipe	29	1.3	5.6	0.2	0.0	0.0	1.5	17	0.5	3	250	33.1
Harvest Vegetable Stir-Fry	½ cup	36	1.8	5.7	0.7	1.2	0.3	1.3	33	0.5	34	344	40.6
Hash Browns	1 cup	60	2.0	13.1	0.0	0.0	0.0	1.0	0	0.0	10	242	0.0
Italian Green Beans	½ cup	26	1.0	5.1	0.2	0.0	0.0	1.7	17	0.7	5	171	21.9
Oven Fried Parmesan Potatoes	⅕ recipe	159	3.2	29.0	3.3	1.0	0.5	2.8	29	1.6	32	484	76.6
Ranch-Style Vegetables	½ cup	49	1.8	9.7	0.3	0.0	0.1	2.2	35	0.6	113	314	48.4
Tomatoes with Yogurt Dressing	½ cup	35	1.2	5.7	0.9	1.3	0.1	1.3	14	0.5	23	260	32.6
Zucchini Garden Casserole	¼ recipe	149	4.5	29.9	1.3	0.0	0.2	3.0	32	1.5	200	637	130.7
SALADS													
Bean and Pasta Salad	1 cup	188	9.4	32.9	2.0	5.1	0.8	3.9	92	2.5	201	298	150.0
Beef, Bean and Pasta Salad (beef)	1 ½ cups	342	22.1	42.7	9.2	44.5	4.0	6.0	213	4.2	390	724	300.0

Note: Ingredients listed as optional are not included in analysis. If a choice of ingredients is given, the first one listed is used.

	Amount	Calories	Protein (grams)	Carbohydrate (grams)	Fat (grams)	Cholesterol (mg)	Saturated Fat (grams)	Dietary Fiber (grams)	Calcium (mg)	Iron (mg)	Sodium (mg)	Potassium (mg)	Phosphorus (mg)
Beef, Bean and Pasta Salad (turkey)	1 1/2 cups	333	21.7	42.7	8.4	40.0	3.2	6.0	218	4.0	393	711	309.0
Black Bean Salad	1/2 cup	81	3.5	15.7	0.4	0.0	0.1	2.4	14	0.9	214	218	65.7
Broccoli Salad	1/2 cup	132	3.8	17.5	5.2	0.1	0.5	2.4	44	1.1	103	272	93.9
Chicken Caesar Salad	1/4 recipe	168	27.9	5.7	3.7	70.6	1.2	2.0	88	2.3	286	534	249.0
Chicken Rainbow Salad	1 1/4 cups	302	20.6	33.9	9.3	42.6	1.1	2.7	73	3.0	225	413	174.0
Citrus Salad	1 1/2 cups	96	2.5	14.5	3.1	0.0	0.4	6.1	68	1.1	9	448	63.7
Confetti Salad	1 cup	128	3.2	26.9	0.9	0.0	0.2	1.9	19	1.0	186	209	90.9
Confetti Shrimp Salad	1/5 recipe	213	22.2	26.9	1.9	177.0	0.4	1.9	55	3.8	388	374	215.0
Frozen Fruit Salad	1/2 cup	80	0.8	18.7	0.2	0.0	0.0	1.4	17	0.5	5	202	15.4
Fruit Cocktail Salad	1/2 cup	57	1.0	13.2	0.0	0.0	0.0	1.0	7	0.2	36	99	30.5
Hawaiian Chicken Salad	1 1/2 cups	294	24.5	27.7	9.4	59.1	1.4	1.6	52	1.8	209	404	240.0
Hot German Potato Salad	1/2 cup	100	2.7	20.2	0.9	0.0	0.1	2.0	16	1.1	88	279	48.0
Mandarin Cottage Salad	3/4 cup	131	13.3	14.0	2.4	4.8	0.6	0.4	110	0.2	435	181	162.0
Mozzarella and Tomato Salad	1/4 recipe	72	4.3	5.3	3.7	8.0	1.6	1.2	99	0.6	90	223	88.7
Rainbow Vegetable Salad	1/6 recipe	200	6.2	33.2	4.8	3.2	0.3	2.7	65	2.5	136	298	71.3
Seafood Pasta Salad	1 cup	157	12.6	18.8	3.5	28.1	1.8	1.2	165	1.1	384	222	213.0
Summer Cole Slaw	1/2 cup	43	1.0	5.6	1.8	0.1	0.1	1.0	38	0.4	51	155	23.0
Taco Salad (beef)	2 cups	323	22.7	33.8	10.8	68.3	4.6	5.8	241	2.8	576	620	288.0
Taco Salad (turkey)	2 cups	313	22.3	33.8	9.8	62.9	3.7	5.8	247	2.6	580	604	298.0
Tuna Macaroni Salad	1 cup	151	16.4	19.5	0.8	23.2	0.2	1.6	31	2.2	408	347	129.0
Turkey Rotini Salad	1 cup	169	16.2	22.0	1.8	29.1	0.5	1.7	27	1.9	151	315	149.0
Vegetable Pasta Salad	1 cup	146	5.0	30.1	0.7	0.0	0.1	1.6	20	1.8	221	200	71.1
Waldorf Salad	1/2 cup	73	0.6	12.1	2.5	0.1	0.2	1.4	21	0.3	70	155	20.6

RICE, BEANS AND PASTA

	Amount	Calories	Protein (grams)	Carbohydrate (grams)	Fat (grams)	Cholesterol (mg)	Saturated Fat (grams)	Dietary Fiber (grams)	Calcium (mg)	Iron (mg)	Sodium (mg)	Potassium (mg)	Phosphorus (mg)
Creamy Dill Fettucini	1/2 cup	183	10.8	28.0	3.2	11.1	1.6	0.7	213	1.7	146	173	182.0

Note: Ingredients listed as optional are not included in analysis. If a choice of ingredients is given, the first one listed is used.

	Amount	Calories	Protein (grams)	Carbohydrate (grams)	Fat (grams)	Cholesterol (mg)	Saturated Fat (grams)	Dietary Fiber (grams)	Calcium (mg)	Iron (mg)	Sodium (mg)	Potassium (mg)	Phosphorus (mg)
Dijon Fettucini	1/2 cup	144	4.4	23.6	3.6	0.2	0.3	0.7	27	1.5	117	87	64.0
Seasoned Black Beans	1/3 cup	103	6.6	18.0	0.4	0.0	0.1	3.1	23	1.6	87	271	106.0
Spanish Rice and Beans	1/2 cup	85	4.2	15.9	0.5	0.0	0.1	2.3	16	0.9	20	155	75.7
Spicy Spanish Rice	1 cup	131	3.4	26.8	1.1	0.0	0.2	1.3	38	1.2	89	299	96.3
Szechuan Pasta	3/4 cup	147	5.7	24.9	2.8	0.0	0.4	1.8	17	1.7	68	167	71.5
SANDWICHES													
Beef and Cabbage Sandwich	1/2	201	16.9	25.1	3.7	32.6	1.1	1.3	97	1.8	285	442	212.9
Black Bean Quesadillas	1/4 recipe	234	12.6	33.8	5.3	10.1	2.0	2.4	188	2.4	377	261	200.0
Broiled Seafood Muffins	2	290	25.9	28.2	8.3	62.0	3.4	0.0	385	1.7	729	327	324.0
Cheese and Chile Quesadillas	1/4 recipe	203	12.2	21.5	7.6	20.2	3.4	0.5	297	1.1	400	66	196.0
Chicken Stir-Fry Sandwich	1/4 recipe	170	16.8	20.4	2.4	34.4	0.6	0.5	46	0.8	210	261	180.0
Chili Dogs	1	249	17.1	34.1	4.9	33.0	1.6	1.2	103	2.8	1097	60	0.0
Garden Deli Sandwich	1	347	14.2	45.5	12.0	19.8	6.3	2.1	111	2.0	690	601	254.0
Ricotta Pizza	1/8 recipe	173	9.1	25.3	4.0	3.6	0.0	0.8	117	0.4	432	113	568.0
Tuna Burgers	1	293	25.8	29.3	8.1	24.9	1.1	0.0	82	3.2	720	309	150.0
Tuna Quesadillas	1/4 recipe	213	18.4	20.3	6.5	22.6	2.1	0.0	176	1.8	446	157	190.0
Turkey Reuben Sandwich	1	311	24.5	34.5	8.3	39.9	3.8	1.5	424	3.0	636	318	356.0
Vegetable Pita Sandwich	1	305	17.1	43.2	7.1	20.2	3.3	2.2	280	0.7	570	493	306.9
Vegetable Stir-Fry Sandwich	1/2	190	7.5	26.3	6.0	10.0	3.2	1.9	65	0.9	333	327	111.0
MEATLESS ENTREES													
Broccoli Quiche	1/8 recipe	129	12.1	11.8	3.6	10.2	1.7	1.2	193	2.1	289	271	165.0
Cheese & Noodle Bake	1/4 recipe	345	20.1	52.5	6.2	21.7	3.2	0.9	361	1.8	274	236	296.8

Note: Ingredients listed as optional are not included in analysis. If a choice of ingredients is given, the first one listed is used.

	Amount	Calories	Protein (grams)	Carbo- hydrate (grams)	Fat (grams)	Choles- terol (mg)	Saturated Fat (grams)	Dietary Fiber (grams)	Calcium (mg)	Iron (mg)	Sodium (mg)	Potas- sium (mg)	Phos- phorus (mg)
Cheese and Tortilla Lasagna	1/6 recipe	220	18.1	28.5	3.7	10.4	1.7	2.4	221	1.7	515	510	307.0
Eggplant Lasagna	1/8 recipe	338	20.2	51.0	5.9	11.8	2.3	3.5	259	3.8	877	231	210.0
Eggplant Parmesan	1/4 recipe	188	11.1	23.6	5.4	16.0	2.9	2.5	245	1.9	623	393	168.0
Harvest Primavera	1/5 recipe	241	9.2	47.3	1.7	1.0	0.4	4.2	74	3.4	341	315	111.0
Italian Curry Pasta	1 1/4 cups	260	9.8	49.1	2.8	2.5	0.8	5.4	84	3.6	89	775	173.0
Pesto Linguini	1 cup	253	8.1	42.3	5.8	1.6	0.9	1.3	34	2.7	76	90	83.2
Rice and Bean Burritos	1/8 recipe	199	6.9	35.9	3.1	0.0	0.5	1.9	72	2.3	226	322	121.5
Sausage Quiche	1/8 recipe	152	14.8	12.2	4.8	5.3	0.9	0.6	138	3.0	452	219	138.0
Spanish Quiche	1/8 recipe	175	13.9	19.2	4.8	10.2	1.7	1.9	192	2.6	475	342	141.0
Vegetable Lasagna	1/8 recipe	309	15.6	51.7	4.5	9.8	2.1	3.6	300	4.4	594	481	242.8

POULTRY

	Amount	Calories	Protein (grams)	Carbo- hydrate (grams)	Fat (grams)	Choles- terol (mg)	Saturated Fat (grams)	Dietary Fiber (grams)	Calcium (mg)	Iron (mg)	Sodium (mg)	Potas- sium (mg)	Phos- phorus (mg)
Aloha Chicken	1/4 recipe	172	25.7	10.4	3.0	69.0	0.8	0.4	25	1.3	104	298	193.0
Black Bean and Chicken Casserole	1 1/4 cups	272	30.6	25.8	5.2	63.3	2.0	2.4	132	1.9	220	413	321.8
Chicken á la King	3/4 cup	214	29.1	15.7	3.9	59.9	1.0	1.5	134	1.8	198	476	273.4
Chicken and Black Bean Burritos	1/6 recipe	239	15.7	35.2	3.9	23.0	0.7	2.8	66	2.4	321	360	181.0
Chicken and Broccoli in Cheese Sce	1/5 recipe	302	33.7	27.4	6.4	68.5	2.7	3.0	309	2.1	276	691	420.1
Chicken and Red Pepper Burritos	1/5 recipe	210	17.2	22.1	5.8	35.7	1.9	0.7	159	1.7	283	234	190.2
Chicken and Stuffing Casserole	1/4 recipe	345	35.2	40.5	4.7	69.0	0.9	1.2	96	3.2	341	565	293.0
Chicken Chop Suey	1 1/4 cups	197	27.7	14.6	3.1	68.3	0.9	2.1	65	1.9	398	630	249.8
Chicken Cordon Bleu	1/4 recipe	218	33.7	7.4	5.9	86.3	2.6	0.3	199	1.4	312	285	299.0
Chicken Curry	1/4 recipe	278	24.4	37.3	3.5	51.7	0.8	3.6	37	1.9	74	447	242.0
Chicken Dijon Fettucini	1 1/3 cups	316	26.7	37.1	6.7	54.3	1.0	1.7	50	3.0	186	340	242.3
Chicken Fricassee	1 cup	216	30.2	14.3	3.2	69.5	0.9	1.6	67	1.8	105	551	257.0
Chicken Hungarian Goulash	1 1/2 cups	315	32.4	38.2	4.0	69.0	1.0	3.6	71	4.3	96	890	296.0
Chicken Medley	1 1/2 cups	220	30.9	17.0	3.2	69.0	0.9	3.7	55	2.0	272	657	255.0

Note: Ingredients listed as optional are not included in analysis. If a choice of ingredients is given, the first one listed is used.

	Amount	Calories	Protein (grams)	Carbo-hydrate (grams)	Fat (grams)	Choles-terol (mg)	Saturated Fat (grams)	Dietary Fiber (grams)	Calcium (mg)	Iron (mg)	Sodium (mg)	Potas-sium (mg)	Phos-phorus (mg)
Chicken Noodle Casserole	1 ½ cups	285	27.4	36.8	3.1	55.2	0.8	1.6	35	3.6	79	372	229.0
Chicken Parmesan	¼ recipe	407	37.3	50.1	6.3	77.0	2.4	3.0	140	4.2	325	381	345.9
Chili Tamale Pie	⅙ recipe	254	15.5	39.0	4.0	29.2	2.1	2.0	126	3.1	572	50	50.6
Creamy Chicken Dijon	¼ recipe	174	25.8	3.1	6.5	69.1	1.0	0.0	29	0.9	202	234	200.0
Patio Chicken and Rice	⅕ recipe	373	34.0	42.5	7.4	83.6	1.9	4.7	102	2.9	293	906	387.0
Ramen Chicken	1 ¾ cups	318	35.0	36.0	3.7	69.0	1.0	2.6	62	3.7	381	726	306.4
Roast Chicken and Vegetables	¼ recipe	405	36.6	39.2	11.3	102.0	2.7	5.4	67	3.1	197	1187	345.0
Skillet Chicken with Tomatoes	1 ½ cups	306	31.5	37.2	3.5	69.0	0.9	4.3	83	3.1	124	1184	295.0
Spanish Chicken	¼ recipe	147	25.8	4.0	3.1	69.0	0.8	1.4	18	1.2	77	342	200.0
Szechuan Chicken	1 ½ cups	232	29.8	8.8	8.6	69.0	1.6	2.8	47	2.0	414	503	256.0
Teriyaki Chicken Breasts	¼ recipe	132	25.4	1.2	2.9	69.0	0.8	0.0	14	0.9	232	218	189.0
Turkey Enchiladas	⅛ recipe	256	21.0	28.6	6.4	34.9	2.3	1.5	228	2.1	352	301	232.7
SEAFOOD													
Bkd Fish and Rice/Dill Chs Sce	¼ recipe	314	37.2	27.3	6.3	58.3	2.8	0.0	360	1.3	290	855	449.0
Barbecued Fish Oriental	¼ recipe	137	23.5	7.3	1.5	41.2	0.3	0.1	42	0.6	357	500	182.6
Creamy Curried Seafood	½ cup	145	25.7	6.7	1.7	42.1	0.4	0.5	83	0.8	76	587	218.0
Creamy Seafood Fettucini	1 cup	310	33.5	31.9	4.2	48.1	1.7	0.7	245	2.1	217	697	368.0
Curried Sole	¼ recipe	147	21.5	1.8	6.0	59.8	0.6	0.2	24	0.7	193	321	310.0
Dijon Fillets	¼ recipe	135	23.5	1.1	4.1	41.6	0.5	0.0	38	0.3	194	475	181.0
Fish Poached in Milk	¼ recipe	118	24.3	1.5	1.6	42.1	0.4	0.0	73	0.2	66	513	209.0
Italian Baked Fish	¼ recipe	142	23.8	8.1	1.5	41.6	0.3	0.3	36	0.7	318	476	182.0
Mushroom Topped Fillets	¼ recipe	122	23.9	2.9	1.6	41.6	0.3	0.6	44	0.7	53	571	204.0
Oriental Seafood	1 ¾ cups	260	30.0	30.2	2.1	41.2	0.4	3.8	70	2.1	328	836	265.7

Note: Ingredients listed as optional are not included in analysis. If a choice of ingredients is given, the first one listed is used.

	Amount	Calories	Protein (grams)	Carbo-hydrate (grams)	Fat (grams)	Choles-terol (mg)	Saturated Fat (grams)	Dietary Fiber (grams)	Calcium (mg)	Iron (mg)	Sodium (mg)	Potas-sium (mg)	Phos-phorus (mg)
Parmesan Fish Fillets	1/4 recipe	182	28.4	8.5	3.9	46.6	1.6	0.3	164	1.4	251	551	254.0
Pasta with Clam Sauce	1/6 recipe	278	14.2	51.5	1.7	14.1	0.2	2.7	76	9.7	46	561	191.0
Seafood Dijon Fettucini	1 1/3 cups	300	25.1	37.1	5.6	32.8	0.6	1.7	68	2.5	179	539	236.6
Seafood Medley	1 1/2 cups	186	28.1	14.3	1.8	41.6	0.4	2.0	90	1.6	226	920	231.0
Seafood Pasta	1/6 recipe	301	26.5	37.6	5.0	38.3	2.3	2.1	200	3.0	144	736	296.5
Shrimp Burritos	1/5 recipe	197	14.6	23.2	5.1	78.1	1.7	0.8	169	2.5	444	217	166.0
Steamed Clams	1/3 recipe	133	21.6	4.8	1.6	56.4	0.1	0.0	87	24.2	98	564	288.0
Stuffed Fish Fillets	1/4 recipe	197	25.5	18.6	2.2	59.8	0.3	0.6	56	1.3	224	453	357.0
Szechuan Seafood	1 1/2 cups	211	27.8	8.8	7.2	41.6	1.1	2.8	70	1.4	405	757	248.0
Tuna Noodle Casserole	1 cup	243	22.3	35.7	1.2	16.8	0.2	2.1	40	3.4	243	335	190.0
Zucchini Fish Bake	1/4 recipe	157	26.0	7.9	2.4	42.8	0.6	1.9	92	1.2	277	705	222.0
BEEF AND PORK													
Baked Stuffed Pork Tenderloin	1/4 recipe	317	31.4	35.0	5.7	65.4	1.4	0.6	73	3.0	297	591	312.0
Beef Hungarian Goulash	1 1/2 cups	321	29.3	37.8	6.1	64.3	2.1	3.6	66	5.8	84	966	286.0
Beef Stroganoff	3/4 cup	187	26.4	8.9	5.1	64.9	1.9	0.8	53	2.9	141	410	241.0
Beef Teriyaki	1/4 recipe	139	22.3	1.2	5.0	64.9	1.9	0.0	9	2.5	220	304	182.0
Ginger Beef	1/2 cup	157	22.4	4.7	5.0	64.9	1.9	0.1	13	2.6	222	315	184.0
Oriental Pork and Noodles	1 3/4 cups	285	30.7	30.3	4.6	65.4	1.5	3.3	40	3.1	360	831	306.0
Pork with Apples and Grapes	1 cup	195	19.1	21.7	3.5	52.4	1.2	1.4	18	1.4	40	461	183.0
Spicy Pork Burritos	1/5 recipe	209	16.4	21.9	6.2	34.3	2.2	0.6	156	1.8	277	276	201.0
Sweet and Sour Pork	1 cup	212	25.8	17.6	4.2	65.4	1.4	2.2	44	1.9	204	744	247.0
Swiss Steak with Rice	1 1/2 cups	316	29.0	36.1	6.2	65.0	2.1	4.3	87	4.2	128	1080	322.6
Szechuan Beef	1 cup	199	22.0	8.3	8.6	52.0	2.2	1.6	45	3.4	323	460	208.0

Note: Ingredients listed as optional are not included in analysis. If a choice of ingredients is given, the first one listed is used.

GROUND MEAT AND SAUSAGE

	Amount	Calories	Protein (grams)	Carbohydrate (grams)	Fat (grams)	Cholesterol (mg)	Saturated Fat (grams)	Dietary Fiber (grams)	Calcium (mg)	Iron (mg)	Sodium (mg)	Potassium (mg)	Phosphorus (mg)
Cornbread Casserole (beef)	1/6 recipe	355	21.2	35.4	14.3	47.1	4.1	3.5	135	3.1	209	443	288.0
Cornbread Casserole (turkey)	1/6 recipe	337	20.4	35.4	12.7	38.1	2.6	3.5	144	2.8	216	416	306.0
Italian Baked Ziti (beef)	1 cup	245	18.8	30.5	5.3	21.3	2.1	2.2	96	2.9	581	175	170.0
Italian Baked Ziti (turkey)	1 cup	238	18.5	30.5	4.7	17.9	1.5	2.2	99	2.8	583	165	177.0
Pasta Olé (beef)	1/4 recipe	315	21.1	34.6	10.2	45.2	4.3	1.7	147	3.4	285	293	221.0
Pasta Olé (turkey)	1/4 recipe	301	20.5	34.4	9.0	38.5	3.2	1.6	154	3.1	287	267	233.0
Pasta Sea Shell Casserole (beef)	1 1/3 cups	297	17.6	38.7	8.0	35.1	2.8	2.9	52	3.9	422	198	126.0
Pasta Sea Shell Casserole (turkey)	1 1/3 cups	284	16.9	38.7	6.8	28.4	1.6	2.9	60	3.7	427	178	139.0
Sausage and Egg Casserole	1/6 recipe	186	20.0	11.7	6.6	36.7	2.7	1.8	264	2.4	650	289	277.0
Sausage and Noodle Bake	1/4 recipe	430	30.0	54.0	10.0	57.6	4.3	0.9	366	2.7	751	342	387.7
Sour Cream Enchiladas (beef)	1/8 recipe	308	21.2	28.6	12.1	45.7	4.6	1.5	224	2.6	359	326	224.0
Sour Cream Enchiladas (turkey)	1/8 recipe	295	20.6	28.6	11.0	39.0	3.5	1.5	231	2.4	364	306	237.0
South of the Border Lasagna (beef)	1/8 recipe	332	24.8	35.1	10.3	42.1	4.0	3.2	202	2.7	426	583	370.0
South of the Border Lasagna (turkey)	1/8 recipe	319	24.2	35.1	9.1	35.4	2.9	3.2	209	2.5	431	562	383.0
Sweet and Sour Beans (beef)	1/2 cup	154	9.4	21.3	3.5	20.8	1.3	5.2	50	2.1	162	578	134.0
Sweet and Sour Beans (turkey)	1/2 cup	148	9.1	21.3	3.0	17.8	0.8	5.2	53	2.0	164	569	140.0
Unstuffed Cabbage Cass (beef)	1 3/4 cups	291	14.9	36.8	9.3	36.5	3.2	0.2	69	2.2	533	603	191.0
Unstuffed Cabbage Cass (turkey)	1 3/4 cups	278	14.3	36.8	8.1	29.7	2.0	0.2	76	2.0	538	583	204.0

DESSERTS

	Amount	Calories	Protein (grams)	Carbohydrate (grams)	Fat (grams)	Cholesterol (mg)	Saturated Fat (grams)	Dietary Fiber (grams)	Calcium (mg)	Iron (mg)	Sodium (mg)	Potassium (mg)	Phosphorus (mg)
Apple Crisp Parfait	1/4 recipe	167	2.3	34.1	2.4	0.9	0.1	1.4	65	0.8	31	215	50.3
Applesauce Bread Pudding	1/9 recipe	118	4.8	22.5	1.0	0.4	0.0	2.9	59	1.2	188	135	100.0
Baked Grapenut Pudding	1/2 cup	126	6.4	24.3	0.4	1.7	0.2	1.1	137	1.7	146	240	147.0

Note: Ingredients listed as optional are not included in analysis. If a choice of ingredients is given, the first one listed is used.

	Amount	Calories	Protein (grams)	Carbohydrate (grams)	Fat (grams)	Cholesterol (mg)	Saturated Fat (grams)	Dietary Fiber (grams)	Calcium (mg)	Iron (mg)	Sodium (mg)	Potassium (mg)	Phosphorus (mg)
Baked Pears with Chocolate Sauce	1 pear	130	0.8	30.0	0.7	0.0	0.1	4.7	26	1.3	10	254	25.8
Banana Cream Pie	1/7 recipe	160	3.6	27.9	3.8	10.8	0.5	0.6	105	0.3	130	264	106.0
Chocolate Cream Pie	1/8 recipe	159	5.3	26.0	3.8	12.2	0.5	0.1	144	0.7	198	302	138.0
Chocolate Peanut Butter Frozen Bars	1 bar	124	4.6	18.0	3.7	1.0	0.8	0.3	81	0.8	189	211	98.0
Chocolate Peanut Butter Pie	1/8 recipe	209	7.2	27.7	7.8	12.2	1.3	0.6	147	0.8	236	359	164.0
Chocolate Vanilla Swirl Pie	1/8 recipe	187	6.8	25.0	6.7	12.0	1.3	0.6	138	0.6	221	295	170.0
Glazed Fruit Cup	1 cup	111	0.8	26.1	0.4	0.0	0.1	2.4	12	0.3	3	181	15.6
New York Cheesecake	1/12 recipe	94	9.5	14.0	0.1	10.0	0.0	0.6	207	0.3	366	74	14.4
Mandarin Yogurt Delight	1/2 cup	40	2.8	6.9	0.1	1.0	0.0	0.3	58	0.1	66	88	28.5
Peach Custard	1/9 recipe	133	3.6	29.3	0.2	0.0	0.0	2.1	16	0.8	46	306	34.5
Peach Popsicles	1	40	0.4	9.7	0.0	0.0	0.0	0.6	3	0.2	3	72	9.9
Pear Custard	1/9 recipe	130	3.1	28.4	0.4	0.0	0.0	2.6	20	0.9	46	159	28.7
Popsicles	1	3	0.5	0.3	0.0	0.0	0.0	0.0	1	0.0	20	0	9.1
Pumpkin Cheesecake	1/12 recipe	86	9.4	11.9	0.1	9.9	0.0	0.4	208	0.5	362	54	15.7
Raisin Bread Pudding	1/9 recipe	141	5.9	26.8	1.1	0.9	0.1	2.8	94	1.3	200	217	132.2
Strawberry Delight	3/4 cup	60	2.5	12.3	0.1	0.7	0.0	1.2	51	0.6	80	169	41.8
Strawberry-Pineapple Shortcake	1/8 recipe	113	2.3	25.4	0.3	0.0	0.0	0.8	48	0.5	221	125	20.1
Strawberry Yogurt Mousse	1/2 cup	49	1.2	7.2	1.7	0.9	0.0	0.9	44	0.1	26	108	15.7

Note: Ingredients listed as optional are not included in analysis. If a choice of ingredients is given, the first one listed is used.

*indicates variation

*indicates variation

*indicates variation

*indicates variation

*indicates variation

*indicates variation

*indicates variation

*indicates variation

*indicates variation

*indicates variation

*indicates variation

Books Available From ScaleDown Publishing:

Quick & Healthy Recipes and Ideas by Brenda J. Ponichtera, R.D.

Quick & Healthy Volume II by Brenda J. Ponichtera, R.D.

To order additional copies of *Quick & Healthy Recipes and Ideas* or *Quick & Healthy Volume II*:

Telephone orders: (541)296-5859 - please have your Visa or MasterCard ready.

Fax orders: (541)296-1875

Postal orders: ScaleDown Publishing, 1519 Hermits Way, The Dalles, Oregon 97058

**Call for quantity (6 or more) discount - for resale only.

— —

Please send me:

———— copies of *Quick & Healthy Recipes and Ideas* at $16.95 each .... $ ————

———— copies of *Quick & Healthy Volume II* at $16.95 each .... $ ————

Shipping & Handling:
$2.50 for the first book and $1.00 for each additional book .... $ ————

Total Enclosed .... $ ————

Payment: ———— Check   ————Visa   ———— Mastercard

Card Number ————————————————— Expiration date ————/————

Name on Card ————————————————— Signature —————————————

— —

Ship to:

Name ——————————————————————————————

Address ————————————————————————————

City ———————————————————— State ———— Zip ————————

Telephone ——————————————————